PROTECTED AREAS AND
INDIGENEOUS
COMMUNITIES

Protected Areas and
INDIGENEOUS
COMMUNITIES

Anthropogenic dependence
& impact on biodiversity

Azra Musavi

PARTRIDGE
A Penguin Random House Company

| ISBN: | Softcover | 978-1-4828-5123-6 |
| | eBook | 978-1-4828-5122-9 |

Print information available on the last page.

To order additional copies of this book, contact
Partridge India
000 800 10062 62
orders.india@partridgepublishing.com

www.partridgepublishing.com/india

For
My Parents

Contents

"Thou Shall Not be Bound by the Tyranny of thy Discipline."

Ramachandra Guha *The Ramachandra Guha Omnibus, 2005*

List of Tables

List of Figures

Acknowledgements

This book is an outcome of my research endeavour for my thesis which I submitted at the Department of Sociology, Aligarh Muslim University and the work which I did as a Senior Research Fellow at the Wildlife Institute of India, Dehradun. My gratitude and sincere thanks to all those who made it possible for me to work in the field of conservation, Mr. H. S. Panwar, Mr. V. B. Sawarkar, Dr. P. K. Mathur, and Dr. V. B. Mathur; sincere thanks to all of them. I would like to thank the staff of the Computer Centre, the Library and AV Section at WII for providing valuable help throughout the project. I would like to thank the Project Tiger staff of Melghat and also the forest staff of Bori. I would specially like to thank Mr. Prakash J. Thosre, Mr Ravi Wankhade, and Mr. Giripuje for providing all possible help and all logistic support. I am also grateful to my field assistants and drivers who provided indispensable help during fieldwork.

I am deeply indebted to my Ph.D. guide, Professor Shad Bano Ahmad, who I am sure would be very happy to see this book. Her positive attitude, support and guidance encouraged me to complete my thesis against all odds.

I would have never known the pleasure of walking in the forest, but for my father, late Prof. A. H. Musavi who

Azra Musavi

introduced me to wildlife and conservation. I am grateful to my parents who supported me in my endeavour.

I am deeply indebted to my friend and mentor, Ainul Hussain who gave me encouragement and direction at times when doing research in an unfamiliar area proved daunting; something he continues to do even today. I would also like to thank all my WII friends for the lively discussions during the course of my work at the institute.

I am grateful to Joe Anderson of Partridge Publications for being immensely patient with me. Thanks are also due to the entire publication and design team at Partridge.

I could not have completed this book but for the encouragement and support of my husband Jamal and my sons Jibran and Ayaan. Thank you for being so caring.

Chapter 1

Introduction

F orest ecosystems, one of the largest repositories of biodiversity, are not only crucial in maintenance of the ecological balance but are also the major sources of fodder, fuel wood and timber. Majority of the developing countries contain the largest chunks of tropical forests which possess over half of the world's floral and faunal species in just 7% of the land area. Forest ecosystems all over the world have however, suffered most in man's quest for development. The decline in the world's forest cover, excluding plantations, has been 13 percent between 1960 and 1990 (Mohapatra, 1999). These forests have been exploited and destroyed at an alarming rate. For example, from an estimated 569 million hectares of forests and woodlots in 1850, tropical Asia lost approximately 76 million hectares till 1950; a reduction of approximately 14% during one century (Thapa and Weber, 1990). The greatest reduction has been in Asia where about 70 percent of the original forest cover has been lost (Mohapatra, 1999).

The scenario has not changed much since 1950. For instance, India lost 4.3 million hectares of forest lands between 1951 and 1980. An appraisal of loss of forest cover showed that approximately 2.6 million hectares of forests have gone to agriculture, 0.5 million hectares to river valley projects and 0.1 million hectares to industries and townships (Lal, 1989). The annual loss of forest cover in India, during 1975 to 1982 was about 13,000 km^2 (Azra, 2012). Needless to say that such large destruction played havoc with India's rich biodiversity. A large number of these plants and animals are endemic to India. However, large scale changes in land use patterns and practices have adversely affected the distribution and abundance of wild animals specially the large and medium sized species. For instance, out of 372 mammalian species found in India, fifty eight have been listed as endangered in Schedule I of Indian Wildlife (Protection) Act (Anon. 1972). Out of these, 18 have no or insignificant populations in protected areas (Rodgers and Panwar, 1988).

The forest ecosystems especially in Africa, Asia and South America, are also under tremendous anthropogenic pressures due to rising human and livestock populations resulting in their degradation (Erickholm, 1975, Upreti, 1987, Pearce *et al.* 1990, Ponting, 1990; Upreti, 1994). The scenario is worst in developing countries where a combination of factors such as large scale commercial exploitation of forests in the past for timber and pulp, clearance of forest land for agricultural purposes to meet the growing needs for food of a soaring human population and unplanned industrialization has led to large scale losses in forest cover. This has resulted in drastic reduction, fragmentation and degradation of wildlife habitats leading to decline in wildlife populations.

Since a very high proportion of human population in developing countries lives below the poverty line, forested areas continue to be degraded as local people exploit them for their everyday needs. The process continues unabated. On the other hand, degradation of forests adversely affects the quality and availability of water, causes increased urban and industrial pollution, in addition to loss of biological diversity. The consequent ecological crisis has resulted in increasing social conflict as different groups exercise competing claims on a dwindling resource base (Guha, 1994).

Conservation of fauna and flora has been an integral part of people's ethics, religious belief and culture in India from time immemorial, for example sacred groves, protecting different wildlife species, etc. Organised forest management however began in 1865 with the major objective of profitable exploitation of timber. This was one of the objectives of the process of converting forests into reserved forests. Most forestry practices in developing countries were guided by the principle of improving economic value of the forests by removing less valuable species. Consequently a large number of trees were replaced by monocultures of timber species. Such policies ignored the role of forests as a major source of livelihood for a large proportion of mostly poor and tribal people, who reside in and around protected areas in most third world countries. The loss of biodiversity has negatively affected the livelihoods of these people (Sunderlin *et al.*, 2005).

By the end of the 19th century game associations started to appear across the country. This movement mainly emphasised avoiding extinction of endangered animals and also regulating hunting of those animals and birds which flourished in safe numbers. The year 1910 witnessed probably the first incidence of shifting people out of a protected area, when the Maharajah of Kashmir ordered the removal of human population from the Dachigam Deer Reserve (Tucker, 1991).

The First World War brought major changes in India. Access to sophisticated weapons, roads and automobiles opened up the far and inaccessible forest areas resulting in increased threats to the country's forests (Phythian-Adams, 1939). To counter this trend, a movement was launched with the Indian National Parks Act becoming a law in 1934 (Tucker, 1991). The Act however, was silent on tribal and peasant populations residing within reserved forests and protected areas. Consequent to this Act, India's first National Park (Corbett Park) was established in the same year, covering 99 square miles of tiger habitat in *Terai* jungles in the Himalayan foothills (Burton, 1951). In 1935 the 'United Provinces Wildlife Preservation Society' organised a major conference of leading wildlife enthusiasts. It was the first organised effort to explore the implications of human presence in and around protected areas *vis-a-vis* their rights of subsistence and self-protection near forests, access to wood and grasses for bona-fide use, poaching and sale of wildlife products both in local and international markets, shifting cultivation, etc. (Burton, 1951).

However, the Second World War brought devastation to wildlife interests as guns flowed into rural India enabling many more peasants to become hunters and poachers (Stracey, 1963). The war also resulted in increased demand for timber leading to accelerated rotational felling schedules. Partition and independence of India in 1947 led to major diversion of forests to cropland in the 1950's, to fulfil the growing demand for agricultural products

(Farmer, 1974). At the same time regional marketing networks and expanding urban centres, particularly in hill regions, exerted new pressures on forest and wildlife zones. The establishment of the National Wildlife Board in 1949 however, led to the declaration of many national parks and protected areas in the 1950's.

With the enactment of Wildlife Protection Act in 1972 (Anon., 1972), serious efforts to conserve India's biodiversity were initiated at the state level. Moreover, the concept of scientific management of protected areas for perpetuation of wildlife gained momentum with the launching of "Project Tiger" in India in 1972. Since then the number of protected areas has increased steadily. Currently there are 85 national parks, 448 sanctuaries and 10 biosphere reserves in India covering approximately 4.2% of the land.

Concept of protected areas

A Protected Area (PA) by definition should be secure from unrestricted use of its resources. The modern concept of conservation is a combination of the two ancient principles of 'resource management' on the basis of accurate inventory and 'protective measures' for ensuring resources from being exhausted. Conservation at times has been considered as a protective 'locking away' of resources by the powerful elite. PAs in reality however play a central role in the social and economic development of rural environments and contribute to the economic well-being of urban centres by reducing the negative effects of resource use (MacKinnon *et al.*, 1986).

In areas outside the PAs people tend to over-exploit natural resources leading to degradation of natural resource base which also affects the water regime. In the long run this leads to serious difficulties for the rural society; as has been witnessed in the Himalayas and other areas too, where over-exploitation of natural resources has resulted in rampant deforestation (accompanied by natural disasters like landslides and floods). This has adversely affected the rural people, especially women who have to walk greater distances to get water, fuel wood and fodder. In the present scenario of high population pressure resulting in degradation and loss of forest lands, interspersing of human habitation in wilderness areas and fragmentation of these areas, most developing countries find it convenient to have several categories of PAs, each with different management objectives and each permitting different levels of manipulation (Rodgers and Panwar, 1988; MacKinnon *et al.*, 1986).

Importance and types of protected areas

Protected areas not only play an important role in a nation's economy by providing a range of benefits, they can also help to meet different objectives ranging from preservation of natural ecological processes to provision of timber, wildlife, water or recreational use at sustainable levels (Dixon and Sherman, 1990).

Though the National Park (NP) is probably the most widely known form of PA, it is only one of many possible categories. In 1959, the IUCN was given the task of maintaining a list of the world's NPs and equivalent reserves. The Commission of National Parks and Protected

Areas (CNPPA) has defined ten categories of conservation areas representing different levels of protection and varying degrees of local, regional and global importance. The classification has eight protected area categories and two international designations *viz.*, Biosphere Reserve and World Heritage Site (IUCN, 1984; MacKinnon *et al.*, 1986). The eight protected area categories are:

Scientific Reserve / Strict Nature Reserve: Their objective is to protect nature and maintain natural processes in an undisturbed state so as to have ecologically representative examples of the natural environment available for scientific study, monitoring and education.

National Park: Their objective is to protect large natural and scenic area of national and international significance for scientific, educational and recreational use.

Natural Monument / Natural Landmark: They aim at protecting and preserving nationally significant natural features because of their unique characteristics of special interest.

Managed Nature Reserve / Wildlife Sanctuary: This category aims at ensuring the natural conditions necessary to protect nationally significant species, groups of species, biotic communities, or physical features of the environment requiring human intervention for their perpetuation.

Protected Landscape: They aim at maintaining nationally significant natural landscapes having a harmonious interaction between people and land, at the same time providing opportunities for recreation and tourism within the lifestyle and economic activity of these areas.

Resource Reserve: Their objective is to protect an area's natural resources for future use and curbing any development activity that could adversely affect the resources.

Natural Biotic Area / Anthropological Reserves: They allow societies living in harmony with the environment to continue their way of life undisturbed by modern technology.

Multiple-use Management Area / Managed Resource Area: In this PA category the conservation of nature is oriented to the support of economic activities, e.g., sustained production of water, timber, wildlife, pasture and outdoor recreation.

The two international PA designations are:

Biosphere Reserves: These are sites of exceptional richness with respect to the diversity and integrity of biotic communities of plants and animals within natural ecosystems.

World Heritage Sites: These are unique natural and cultural sites having outstanding universal significance.

Protected areas in India

The Wildlife Protection Act and the Indian Forest Act allow several levels of protection (Rodgers and Panwar, 1988), under the following categories:

National Park: In a NP no consumptive utilisation of land or natural resources is permitted except for management to achieve conservation objectives. This category, in theory, is the ultimate level of protection that can be given to an area.

Wildlife Sanctuary: The conservation of biological values in a wildlife sanctuary holds priority over resource utilisation such as timber, fuel wood, minor produce harvesting and livestock grazing.

Reserved Forest and Protected Forest: The principle objective of these is the maintenance of forest resources. However, while reserved forest allows less intensive produce collection or grazing, in a protected forest local pressures are higher. Although both reserved and protected forests cannot provide long term conservation of important wildlife resources, such forest cover is important as buffer and corridor area.

Game Reserve / Wetland Reserve: This category was important in the past when game hunting was permitted. However, now it is an uncommon category because there are legal restrictions on hunting.

Closed Area: This category can be used to give protection to selected species in government forests, especially in areas without adequate government land. However, it has no control over the prevalent land-use practice and therefore, cannot guarantee the existence of suitable habitat for target species.

Biosphere Reserve: These are ideally large planning areas which are integrated ecosystems containing legally protected core zones such as parks and sanctuaries within a framework of human settlement and resource exploitation areas. The Government of India proposed that examples of the country's richest and most distinctive biomes be given extra attention as biosphere reserves.

Sacred Forest Groves of North-East India and Western Ghats: In both North Eastern India, as well as, in the Western *Ghats* traditional resource conservation or sacred groves are losing their status due to growing population and the younger generation's lack of interest in their traditional heritage. Long-term conservation of these areas would however, require additional legal status.

Chapter 2

Issues in Forest Conservation

The impact of anthropogenic activities on the environment in general and forests in particular have received great deal of attention all over the world resulting in a large amount of literature on the subject. While lamenting the disappearing forests and resulting desertification of formerly productive natural ecosystems the inappropriate anthropocentric activities are held responsible for their conversion into less productive desert like ecosystems especially of Lebanon and Syria (Ponting, 1990). A similar view is held by several others who have discussed this ongoing process throughout the world, especially in Africa, Asia and South America (Erickholm 1975; Upreti 1987; Pearce *et al.*, 1990). Large land settlement projects in Asian, African and Latin American countries are also a major cause for deforestation (Thapa and Weber, 1988). Other causes of deforestation are colonization of tropical Asian countries, leading to exploitation of their forests by the Europeans for their requirements; expansion of agricultural land through land grabbing or encroachments by local people; and shifting cultivation in its present form (Thapa and Weber, 1990). Lal (1989) too has blamed diversion of forest land to other uses, for the destruction of forests in India. Bajracharya (1983) and Blaikie (1985) have identified increasing landlessness and marginalisation of farmers as the factors which have compelled people to encroach on forest lands along with intensifying land-use.

According to McNeely (1990) natural resource depletion in developing and underdeveloped countries is more of a consequence of foreign demand than local consumption since globalisation results in far reaching impacts of any policy or action. This argument is supported by Upreti (1994) who holds responsible the American and European transnational corporations operating in Third World countries for massive destruction of forests and other natural resources. Myres (1981), Uhlig (1984) and Thapa and Weber (1990) also agree that the alarming trends of destruction of tropical moist forests in South and South-east Asia are due to the rapidly rising demand for timber in developed countries. Moreover growing population, urbanisation, industrialisation and illicit felling at large scale in developing countries, have also been considered as factors leading to deforestation. Several reports and papers (GOI, 1976 and 1982; Haimendorf, 1982) on the other hand, have drawn attention to the extent of forests being affected annually by shifting cultivation and the seriousness of the situation in various parts of the country. Destructive effect of shifting cultivation is a recent phenomenon caused due to the deterioration of the socio-economic situation of the forest dwellers as result of deforestation (Fernandes *et al.*, 1988).

At times both ecologists and social scientists hold economic development responsible for strong adverse impact on conservation activities (Dasmann *et al.*, 1973; Myres, 1981). Studies have shown linkages between threats to environmental conservation and stages of

economic development (Machlis and Tichnell, 1987).
All these authors agree that protected areas in particular,
are vulnerable to significant ecological changes resulting
from industrialisation, intensified agriculture, forestry,
mining and other economic development projects in and
adjacent to these parks. Hart (1966), Forester (1973),
Nelson (1978) and Blower (1984) follow a similar line
of argument. According to their studies, socio-economic
characteristics of the region determine the type and
intensity of threats to the parks.

Environmental degradation is considered the outcome of
imbalances in costs and benefits of conservation and lack
of coordination between the various agencies / institutions
responsible for policy-making and implementation (Pearce,
1975; Clark and Munn, 1986; Perrings, 1987; McNeely,
1988). Land-use policies and management strategies
also have negative effects on biodiversity (Rodgers,
unpublished data). According to him, silvicultural and
management systems in India have been guided by the
principle of improving the economic value of the forests
by removing less valuable species. This has resulted in loss
of biodiversity. Forest exploitation by local people for fuel,
fodder, grazing and NTFPs has also been considered as
another factor responsible for this. Nearby residents who
depend on the resources of a PA are considered by some to
pose a greater threat to its conservation, than development
projects (Dixon and Sherman, 1990). Therefore economic
forces are considered effective protection tools to motivate
local communities to change the existing resource-use
patterns to more sustainable levels.

Though the field of economic valuation of natural
resources underwent changes there were difficulties in

measuring the true economic values of PAs (Dixon and Sherman, 1990) which have been partly responsible for the contribution of natural resources to a nation's well-being. Moreover, there were also conceptual difficulties in quantifying various intangible services of the Forestry Sector and including them in the GNP computations (Pant, 1977). Various studies have also discussed the contribution of forest resources to India's NNP and GDP as well as the relatively low returns from India's forests (Sarin & Khanna, 1981; Gupta and Guleria, 1992).

Protected Area – People Conflicts

Over the years PAs have been established in most countries to provide protection to endangered biodiversity. Not all PAs were however successful in achieving conservation objectives, especially the ones located in heavily populated landscapes. There are various view-points to this issue. Some studies point to the major lacunae in planning a PA in terms of overlooking human needs and aspirations of the local population and the lack of and / or inadequacy of mechanism to deal with ensuing conflicts (Durbin and Ralambo, 1994). Relations with local people are also considered to be of paramount importance for effective PA management. This view point is supported by several others who have given examples of conflicts between local communities and PAs throughout the world wherever these areas have been created without addressing local people's social, political and economic needs and aspirations and their long-term viability (Lusigi, 1981; Abel and Blaikie, 1986; Carew-Ried, 1990; Talbot and Olindo, 1990). In developing countries these problems are further magnified due to rapidly growing populations which put increasing pressures on fragile ecosystems on one hand, while on the other, the governments do not have adequate resources to invest in these PAs (Hannah, 1992).

Studies have also highlighted the negative side of establishing a PA in people-dominated landscapes especially when people have to be relocated and access to the PA resources is denied or curtailed (Brechin *et al.*, 1991; Raval, 1991). This not only affects the attitudes of the local people towards the PA but also causes adverse social impacts to residents. The local poor communities are most adversely affected by exclusionary policies of NP and PAs, as they depend on the PA resources for their daily subsistence and domestic commodity production needs. Therefore, it is necessary to take into consideration the social and economic structure of the region when planning a PA or displacing the resident communities. Several studies also agree that disregard for tribal people and their land rights is not only one of the greatest injustices in most third world countries but also a fundamental issue with a bearing on some of the current problems of colonisation of tribal lands and exploitation of forests for foreign exchange by a powerful minority (Guppy, 1980; Goodland and Irwin, 1975; and Davis, 1977).

The injustice caused to local indigenous communities at times leads to conflicts. For instance the establishment of Royal Chitwan National Park and imposition of regulations restricting the use of its resources by local people resulted in conflicts between the PA management and the people (Nepal and Weber, 1994). Such restrictions which curtail traditional rights of people to an area lead to illegal activities like poaching, logging and hunting which are justified by them on the ground of threat by wild animals to their lives, livestock and crops (Milton and Binney, 1980; Mishra, 1982; Lehmkuhl *et al.* 1988, Nepal and Weber, 1993). There are also conflicts between local societies and the PAs due to crop depredation by large ungulates and man-eating and cattle lifting by predators like tigers and leopards (Saharia, 1984; Schelhas, 1991). In a study on PA-people relationships in Kenya's Amboseli NP (Shelton, 1983) it was found that at times protection given to a PA and its wildlife may result in direct hardships to the local people due to increasing wildlife populations. While at the same time, the people might want to continue exercising their traditional rights on these forests. Although there are substantial benefits in terms of recovery of plant cover leading to reduction in flooding and soil erosion as well as provision of employment opportunities in the park for the local people. Therefore, an understanding of the causes of conflicts among the users of the natural resources is imperative if PA-people conflicts and environmental degradation are to be reduced. Moreover, mechanisms to resolve user conflicts and balancing competing interests are essential for developing special area management (Brower and Carol, 1987).

Economics and Conservation

At a macro-level, economics can play an important role in achieving the objectives of conservation, as economics can be used to direct government policies for promoting sustainable development (McNeely, 1990). There is an urgent need for designing government policies which would minimise deforestation, desertification and destruction of habitats and species etc. (Upreti, 1994). This can be achieved by integrating resource accounts in national accounting to represent the real costs of development in economic decision-making. This would give a more accurate picture of the effect of economic policies on ecological systems (Barbier, 1987; Repetto, 1992). These opinions are in contrast to traditional economic analysis which was mostly developed during the Great Depression and was therefore, more concerned with direct economic issues rather than with economic valuation of natural resource stocks.

At the micro-level, the importance of local people's participation and project design is essential for achieving community based management (Kiss, 1990; Brechin *et al.*, 1991; Wells *et al.*, 1992). Moreover, it is argued that conservation strategies are more successful when they are worked out in a true co-management framework (Pinkerton, 1987). Consequently, they are viewed as 'more legitimate' by the local people. It is rightly emphasised that there is a need for understanding the external situations affecting a PA (Schelhas, 1991) and the management of a PA should be tailored to effectively address the adjacent land and local people's issues. The park management cannot be indifferent to the resource needs and perceptions of local people and there is a need to understand both the natural resource and the neighbouring people (Rodgers, 1991). Therefore, a joint or participatory management of the PA is a better option.

Findings of a study on Shoolpaneshwar Sanctuary in India also supported this argument (Sarabhai, *et al.*, 1991). The study brought forth the necessity to develop the concept of Joint Sanctuary Management (JSM) on the lines of Joint Forest Management (JFM). It was felt that such an approach would not only enable the local resident communities to continue living within the sanctuary, but also involve them in planning and protection of the PA. At the same time this can be made into a paying proposition for the local communities by providing them with incentives. There is also need for strengthening the PA-people relationship by involving the tribes in generation and protection of forests through sharing of usufruct and by providing gainful employment to them (Tewari, 1991). Thus the forestry sector must act as a nodal agency for alleviating poverty.

The importance of tackling rural poverty of local communities as an important component of conservation planning was also emphasised by IUCN's World Conservation Strategy (1980). For examples Annapurna Conservation Area Project links conservation with quality of life issues and basic needs of the people living in the mountainous region of Nepal (Bunting and Sherpa, 1991). As far as the external issues facing the PA management are concerned there is a need to allow the local people controlled access to some of the PA resources to meet the people's critical resource needs (Schelhas, 1991; Lehmkuhl *et al.*, 1988). It is further felt that this would also help in improving relations between PA management and local communities. Sharing of information by all institutions involved and evolving a consensus between stake holders on development objectives should be used as a means of achieving conservation objectives (McNeely, 1990).

Furthermore the need for co-operation, equity and understanding of ecological and social sustainability for achieving environmental conservation has also been emphasised (Upreti, 1994). The importance of cultural and ecological factors for sustainable development and benefits in terms of financial gain, improved social services, and energy benefits is also important (Lusigi, 1981; Barbier, 1987; Durbin and Ralambo; 1994). Some studies also lay emphasis on the socio-economic context and ethical aspects of the neighbouring people and the conservation of natural resources (Saharia, 1984; de Blohm, 1992; Upreti, 1994). At times the local or regional political factors also influence the uneven development and underdevelopment of an area (Simon, 1989).

While local people depend on the resources of PAs for most of their necessities like thatch, timber, firewood, leafy fodder and supplementary grazing by livestock (Nepal and Weber, 1993; Sharma and Shaw, 1993) there is a need to assess the access to opportunities like non-farm employment, marketing support, agricultural extension including veterinary services as means of reducing pressure on and destruction of forests (Thapa and Weber, 1990). Studies have suggested reducing or diverting demand to products with alterative sources (Guppy, 1980) as well as ways of mitigating the resulting conflicts between man and forests (Eidswik, 1980). It is argued that conservation and development can be achieved by increasing financial support to PAs. Moreover, encroachments on forest lands also make them vulnerable to degradation especially forests near habitations are subjected to indiscriminate grazing, lopping, over-felling, fires, etc., resulting in depletion of growing stock (Singh, 1981).

There is need for setting up areas which allow controlled exploitation of some resources as it is difficult to justify the existence of PAs in developing countries *vis-a-vis* the economic needs of the people (Shelton, 1983). This is because the benefits from PAs are not only inconspicuous but are available only in the long run. The concept of PA in developing countries is at times critically viewed as "locking away precious resources", while the majority suffers under poverty and starvation (Brechin *et al.*, 1991). On the other hand, eco-development in protected areas can help bring benefits like grasses, fruits and employment opportunities to the local people. Over the years the buffer zone concept has been evolved as an area of controlled and sustainable land-use separating a PA from direct biotic pressures and at the same time providing benefits to local rural communities (MacKinnon *et al.*, 1986; Orsdol, 1987; Ishwaran and Erdeleu, 1990). More recently buffer zones have been considered as areas with restrictions on resource-use or where special development measures are undertaken for enhancing their conservation value (Sayer, 1991). The buffer zone concept has been used in Royal Chitwan National Park for reducing park-people conflicts (Nepal and Weber, 1994).

Dependence on Forests

Out of the various resources for which local communities depend on the PAs, fuel wood extraction, its effects and consumption patterns seem to have got a lot of attention, especially in India. Fuel wood which is a major cooking and heating medium in the entire rural sector as well as in a large part of the urban areas is considered as one of the major causes of deforestation (Fernandes *et al.*, 1988) and destruction of forests in developing countries (Lanly, 1982) with almost all rural households in developing countries using fuel wood for cooking food and heating houses. Increase in population and deteriorating economic conditions therefore cause increase in fuel wood consumption. Exploitation of forests for fuel wood in developing countries of Africa and Asia is considered as a major cause of accelerating the degradation of forests leading to land degradation in the watersheds (Osemeobo, 1988; Bowonder *et al.*, 1987; Thapa and Weber, 1990; NES, 1992).

Fuel wood consumption is considered responsible for reckless exploitation of natural resources and land degradation (Purohit and Trivedi, 1991). A study carried out in North-east India also has blamed the use of fuel wood as a primary energy source, for causing severe deforestation in the region (Maikhuri, 1991). It is further argued that this pattern has in turn affected the supplies of fuel wood, fodder and fertilizer for the farm-household economies (Thapa and Weber, 1994). According to a report of FAO (1984), 90% of all energy consumed was from wood out of which 65% was for domestic purposes. Moreover, up to 99% of the fuel wood consumed was harvested from indigenous forests and bush land. It was found that harvesting was heavy in areas near major settlements, urban centres and along some roads where charcoaling occurs. This finding is supported by others who have argued that, while it is the forest dwellers who are often accused of over-exploiting the forests, all the firewood collected by them is not for local consumption, but for meeting the fuel requirements of the urban consumer (Fernandes *et al.*, 1988). Poverty was considered as an important factor which forces the forest dwellers to depend on fuel wood sale for their survival. Moreover, fuel wood demand by urban households is considered as an important factor which encourages landless and marginal farmers resort to fuel wood collection from forests for selling in market centres as it provides them with additional income for meeting their subsistence needs (Thapa and Weber, 1991; Adhikari, 1988). In Nepal and India where majority of the population stays in rural areas around urban centres, fuel wood collection and sale can form a lucrative enterprise for the villagers (Bowander *et al.*, 1987; Sharma, 1987).

While on one hand use of fuel wood as a major source of energy in developing countries is attributed to free and easy access to forests and to the simple technology of wood-fuel use (Adhikari, 1988). On the other hand, large scale consumption of fuel wood is considered as a factor of poverty (Openshaw, 1980; Wallace, 1981; Eckholm *et al.*, 1984; Blaikie, 1985). They argue that in most of the Asian countries a large percentage of population is poor and subsists on marginal agriculture. Consequently they do not have the resources to obtain alternative sources of energy and are therefore forced to cut trees. Studies have also revealed that for those living at subsistence level there was no viable alternative to fuel wood (Singh, 1981; APROSC, 1983; Sharma, 1987; Sawarkar, *et al.*, 2000). According to these studies, in developing countries most of the poor and a substantial proportion of the middle and upper-middle urban households, depend on fuel wood to fulfil their energy requirement as they cannot afford conventional fuels.

On the basis of the energy-use pattern in rural India, studies have suggested the feasibility of social forestry, commercial fuel wood farming and community forestry schemes for establishing village fuel wood forests (Kaul and Gurumurti, 1981). Emphasis has also been given to the need for a suitable energy policy (Singh, 1981). Fuel wood studies in Java have also concluded that agro-forestry based fuel wood production can successfully meet the fuel wood demands of millions of households; the main sources of fuel wood in Java are forested land, tree crop estates and private land (Smiet, 1990).

Over the years several studies were carried out to relate domestic fuel wood consumption in rural areas to various socio-economic factors (Sagar, *et al.*, 1981, Maithani, *et al.*, 1986, Negi, *et al.*, 1986 and Misra, *et al.*, 1988). It was found that socio-economic variables like family size, settlement pattern, caste groups and landholding, were associated with fuel wood consumption (Purohit and Trivedi, 1991). The household size was found to be directly related to quantity of firewood consumed (Mahendra *et al.*, 1992). It has however been observed that enhanced use of alternative sources of energy can balance the increasing demand of fuel wood and make use of fuel more economic (Maithani *et al.*, 1986). Studies have also examined the fuel wood consumption patterns in four tribal communities under varying ecological and socio-cultural conditions in North-east India (Maikhuri, 1991). Moreover, studies on relation between distance from forest and domestic fuel wood consumption in hilly areas, found that distance from forests had a significant effect on total and per capita firewood consumption (Mahendra *et al.*, 1992).

Studies have also been carried out to find the effect of both distance from forest and socioeconomic variables on fuel wood consumption. It was found that increase in the distance travelled for collecting fuel wood due to deforestation led to decreased collection (Fernandes *et al.*, 1988). The study also revealed that areas close to the villages were monopolised by the upper classes and therefore, the poorer classes had to go far from the villages for collecting firewood. An empirical study of household fuel wood consumption in the hills analysed the effect of distance from forest, household size, annual income, land and livestock holding (Mahendra *et al.*, 1992). The study also revealed that fuel wood was collected from neighbouring forests by the rural people for as this did not incur any cost to them, except the labour involved in collecting and carrying it.

Over the years, studies have also been carried out on various aspects of non-timber forest produce (NTFP), which is another major resource being extracted from the forests mostly by the local people. It was rightly emphasised there was a need for 'action research' for better management of NTFPs (Sarin, 1981). Some studies found a class-based dependence on NTFPs (Fernandes *et al.*, 1988), as while most of the NTFPs were collected by upper classes it was the weaker sections which depended for their survival on these in the lean season. There have also been studies on the interaction and relationships between the tribal communities in Kodikanal (Tamil Nadu, India) and the surrounding forests (Kennedy, 1991). Over the years the literature on dependence on forests for NTFPs and their contribution to household incomes has grown manifold (Sunderlin *et al.*, 2005; Mamo *et al.*, 2007; Babulo *et al.*, 2009).

The possibility of employment generation through collection, processing and sale of NTFPs has also been explored by several authors. For example, NTFPs accounted for employment generation of more than 1 million man-years or over 55% of the total employment in the forestry sector (Pant, 1977). There was possibility of employment generation for the rural unemployed in the forestry sector, especially the NTFPs (Gupta and Guleria, 1992). Moreover, according to the study the contribution of forestry sector could be increased by giving more attention to exploitation and marketing of NTFPs.

Yet another form of dependence on forest is for livestock grazing. This has got a lot of attention in the tropical countries as it is considered one of the major causes of degradation of forests. Increasing livestock numbers along with conversion of forest lands to agricultural land were considered responsible for adversely affecting the regenerative capacity of forests (Thapa and Weber, 1990). Financial and infrastructural constraints had led to the small farmers increasing the numbers of those livestock species which had a low per unit cost, e.g. goats, sheep etc. It was however noted that, foraging by these medium-sized animals severely affected forest regeneration. Increasing fragmentation of land and marginalisation of farmers has led to the farmers increasing their livestock inventory to complement their insufficient crop production (Sheikh, 1986). Rising market prices of livestock products, unavailability of farm fodder and inadequate veterinary and extension services were also responsible for increasing livestock numbers and consequent pressure on forests (Thapa and Weber, 1990; Sheikh, 1986). This had made pastoralism a lucrative business both for the farmers and as well as for the pastoralists.

Moreover, non-availability of non-farm employment opportunities and lack of agricultural support facilities have led to the people increasing the number of their livestock holdings (Bajracharya, 1983; Blaikie, 1985).

Studies have also found that social status and economic prosperity also play a role in large livestock holdings in most tropical Asian countries (Hudson, 1980; Fenerstein *et al.*, 1987; WRI and IIED, 1987). Increase in livestock numbers in developing countries were thus an outcome of both economic and social factors (Thapa and Weber, 1990; Sheikh, 1986).

Ecologists on the other hand differ from social scientists regarding the factors responsible for over-grazing (Homewood and Rodgers, 1987). While the ecologists view it as the outcome of traditional patterns of communal land tenure and individual herd ownership (Lamprey, 1983 and Hardin, 1968). Social scientists attribute it to external constraints like loss of rangelands to other forms of land-use (Hjort, 1982), or breaking down of traditional controls under external influence (Sandford, 1983; Little, 1981), and unavailability of farm-fodder which has put constraints on stall-feeding resulting in free uncontrolled grazing (Mahat, 1987).

Grazing by domestic livestock has attracted a great deal of attention in terms of its effects on plant species, along with the destructive effects of pastoralist grass fires and tree felling (Lamprey, 1983). Grazing is considered to impact not only plants but also ground cover, soil structure, water availability and rainwater infiltration (Kelly and Walker, 1976). Studies found livestock grazing combined with fodder collection as the major cause of destruction and degradation of forest resources in the Middle Hills of Nepal (Fox, 1983). While some studies have found that short-term changes in plant species composition and abundance can be easily demonstrated (Sandford, 1983), others have found it difficult to establish the relative importance of grazing regime versus other factors as ecological studies were of more recent and short-term nature (Homewood and Rodgers, 1987).

Carrying capacity of different forests and rangelands, type of grass and tree vegetation and its growth characteristics also played a role in determining the extent of impact of grazing (Thapa and Weber, 1990). They state that when the size of livestock herds exceeds the carrying capacity of the land it results in severe forest and grass destruction. Studies on the comparative carrying capacities of open grasslands and forests in Nepal and India, found that the stocking rates (of domestic livestock) in both the countries were several times greater than the carrying capacity of their open grassland and forest (Mahat, 1987). For example, in India they were greater by 10 times in open grasslands and 5 times in forests. Under these conditions regeneration of forest and grass resources is considered unfeasible.

Women and Forests

There is a special symbiotic relationship between women and the environment, especially in the third world countries. Rural women have been characterized as 'farmers of the living landscape' whose 'landscape midwifery' from the Amazon Basin to the Sahel to the Himalayas provides food, fuel, medicine, water, shelter, fodder and fertilizer and a cultural umbilical cord to their communities (Rocheleau, 1992). Moreover, many of these women have had to take up work and responsibilities often because of the male out migration and civil strife. These responsibilities had traditionally been in the male domain.

However, these women lack legal rights to access and control over resources and policies.

The role of women in NTFP collection has also received growing attention over the years (Sarin and Khanna, 1981) and rightly so as they are considered the primary users of biodiversity resources since in most cases it is the women who collect not only fuel wood but also majority of NTFPs. With studies ranging from women's dependence on forests & participation in joint forest management (Das, 2011) to women's resource rights (Vasan, 2007) and effects of deforestation on women's work burden (Mishra and Mishra, 2012) the field is ever expanding. There has also been a growing interest in women's role in conserving biodiversity (Abramovitz and Nicholas, 1992; Agarwal, 1992 and 2010; Baker and Barnes, 2010).

Any unsustainable exploitation of natural resources has direct implications for women because they are responsible for providing water, food, fuel wood and fodder and in doing so they interact closely with their natural surroundings (Anon., 2002). As primary resource users, these women do much of the hard work needed to maintain or restore the surrounding environment. The irretrievable loss of biodiversity all over the world is diminishing human welfare and closing the options for the future (Abramovitz and Nichols, 1992). This loss can only be stopped through full participation of women in sustainable development and conservation of nature.

Environmental degradation is often both a cause and an effect of the lifelong hardship of rural women in developing countries. Ecological destruction and marginalization of women are the inevitable results of most development programmes (Shiva, 1988) as they fail to take into account the contributions of women as natural resource managers. This has led to both biotic and human impoverishment. Majority of world's population, most of whom are women and children, are so poor that mere subsistence is a daily struggle. Maurice Strong in an address to the *World Women's Congress for a Healthy Planet* (November, 1991) reiterated that "poverty has a gender bias ... women and children are the prime victims of unsustainable development". Women's role is however, seldom recognized.

Women who have been the victims of this form of development have most of the times stood up to protect and preserve nature and their survival. Indian women have also been taking initiatives to protect and conserve forests, land and water whose destruction has led to their marginalization in the Indian society as well as in the economy, especially so of the lower income strata and in rural areas (Shiva, 1988). The Chipko Movement was supported by the women of the Garhwal region in India. The word '*Chipko*' means hugging the trees to save them from being cut down. The women in the region realised the negative impacts of rampant tree cutting in the villages due to the nexus between the contractors and forest department. The negative impacts were not only in the form of loss of resources like fuel wood and fodder, but also had negative ecological effects like floods, loss of top soil, etc. The women in the Garhwal region supported the protests initiated by social activists like Chandi Prasad Bhat and Sunder Lal Bahuguna and consequently the Chipko movement spread across a large number of villages in the hills (Guha, 2005).

Forest – People Relationship

The relationship between protected areas and the local communities have been the focus of several studies. Example from Annapurna Project suggests that park-people relationships can be improved by fulfilling the daily needs of indigenous people through sustainable use of natural resources like firewood and fodder (Bunting & Sherpa, 1991). Government policies should also take into consideration the problems of the landless people and explore viable alternatives for them in order to reduce pressure on forests (Upreti, 1994). Furthermore, if dependence of local communities can be met through viable solutions, it would help in improving the park-people relationship between local people and protected area management (Shelton, 1983; Sarabhai *et al.*, 1991).

India too has rich folk traditions of conservation of biodiversity as well as sustainable use of natural resources for example, protecting *Pipal* (Ficus) trees or even whole communities of trees in the system of sacred groves. These woodlots are referred to as the safety forest or supply forest by the local people (Gadgil, 1991). Unfortunately, the governments, forest departments and the wealthy appropriated sacred groves, village woodlots and other communal lands, undermining time-honoured traditions that conserved natural resources as they felt justified in releasing the locked-up capital of over mature timber in the sacred groves or reclaiming land for industrialization, urbanization, or for developing infrastructure for the growth of the economy (Gadgil 1991; Abramovitz and Nichols, 1992).

The Chipko movement was another people's movement organised by local villagers to protect the Garhwal forests from the Government, Forest Department and Contractor nexus. The heavy monsoon of 1970 caused devastating floods in the Garhwal region leading to considerable loss of life. According to Guha (2005) the 1970 flood marked a turning point in the ecological history of the region. The villagers began to perceive the links between deforestation, landslides and floods. The Dashauli Gram Swarajya Sangh (DGSS) co-operative organised a demonstration in Chamoli district. One of the demands was 'priority to the local use of forests' (Guha, 2005). In 1973, a private company was allotted ash trees in Mandal forest. This resulted in meetings to discuss the ways to protest against commercial use of forest. Chandi Prasad Bhatt suggested 'emracing the trees' (Chipko) as a way of protecting them (Guha, 2005, p. 157, "The Unquiet Woods: Ecological Change and Peasant Resistance in the Himalaya"). The villagers of Mandal, led by their headman resolved to hug the trees to protect them. This was the beginning of a series of protests by the villagers of Garhwal region to protect their forests.

Chapter 3

Melghat and Bori

The *Satpura* hills (better known for Hora hypothesis) in the Central highlands of India is a region with a vast conservation potential *vis-á-vis* some highly endangered species such as tiger, threatened by the high dependence of local people on these forests. The *Satpura* Conservation Area (SCA) located in the *Satpura* hills is protected under a cluster of four PAs *viz*., Melghat Tiger Reserve (1597 km²) in Maharashtra and Bori Wildlife Sanctuary (486 km²), Satpura National Park (524 km²), Pachmarhi Wildlife Sanctuary (417 km²) in Madhya Pradesh. The forests of SCA are a source of livelihood for a large number of people (tribal and non-tribal communities) and livestock living inside these forests. Moreover, these forests are also under anthropogenic pressures from much larger human and livestock populations residing around these PAs.

Although no long-term ecological studies have been carried out in either of the protected areas, they have been a source of interest to biologists for a long time (Hora, 1937 a). In his papers on geographical distribution of Indian fresh water and Himalayan fishes, Hora (1937a & 1937b) has tried to explain the reason behind the similarity in the species found in these forests and those of the east Himalayan, Indo-Chinese and Indo-Malayan regions. In Bori forests a floristic survey was conducted by State Forest Research Institute (SFRI), Jabalpur. Apart from this Sawarkar and Panwar (1987) wrote about the need for an integrated strategy of land-use for the *Satpura* Conservation Area. Also, Sawarkar and Uniyal (unpublished data) wrote about the diversity of the *Satpura* hills.

Melghat comparatively has had more attention focused on it, probably because it was declared a Tiger Reserve in 1972. Therefore, research especially on its flora has been carried out in great detail (Patel, 1982; Dhore & Joshi, 1988). A study on aspects of predation on domestic livestock by tigers in Melghat Tiger Reserve was carried out by Sawarkar (1979) during 1973 to 1976, followed by Wankhade and Mahajan (1992) on the same aspect. Ladkat and Chopkar (1992) wrote about the people in Melghat, their ethnic identities and dependence on forest. Gogate (1992) wrote about the need to regulate grazing by domestic livestock in the interest of wildlife management goals. A Grazing Settlement Report which was submitted before Gogate's management plan, while calculating the available area for grazing and the carrying capacity of the reserve did not take into consideration either the wild herbivore populations or the inaccessibility of certain areas and terrains, both to livestock and wildlife.

As far as tribal or people related studies are concerned, several anthropometric studies have been conducted by Gorlitzer, V. along with Koppers, W. and Fuchs, S. in 1939 on the Korkus of Melghat. The findings of this study were analysed and published by Weninger (1952). Chattopadhyay (1941), Basu (1970) have also worked on Korkus of Melghat region. Fuchs (1972) has done an anthropometric analysis of both Korkus and Nahals of Melghat. In addition to these studies, short surveys in Melghat villages have also been carried out by colleges and universities in the *Vidharba* region, especially after the starvation deaths in 1984. However, as far as family structure and organisation are concerned no studies have been carried out on these parameters in either Melghat or Bori. Therefore, no empirical data is available on effect of change in forest on the family life of the local inhabitants for the two study areas.

History and past management practices

Not much historical information is found on this region except in the detailed account by Forsyth (1889), Russell and Lal (1975) and the various working plans of these forests. In the 16th century, a highway between upper India and the Deccan through the *Satpura* hills opened the country to the immigrants, who monopolised the rich arable areas, now known as *Berars*. Consequently, the local inhabitants, the *Gonds*, were forced to retreat to the higher plateaus of central hills (the *Gondwana* highlands), where they practised shifting cultivation until the establishment of the British power in the region in the year 1818 (Fuchs, 1988). Thereafter they were encouraged by the British to settle down in permanent villages within the forests where they have been practising subsistence agriculture.

In due course a railway line was laid through the region and in 1861 the *Gondwana* highlands were consolidated into the Central Provinces, primarily for economic reasons. These forests were capable of supplying good quality timber and black soil which produced cotton required by the Manchester cloth industry. The wealth of this region was recognised and one of the first steps taken by the administration of the Central Provinces was the organisation of a Forest Department in 1862, for the detailed examination and conservation of the timber bearing areas.

Before the Melghat *tahsil* came under British administration in 1853, the forests were being exploited by the local inhabitants, the *Korkus*, for trade in forest produce. Moreover, large areas in this tract were under shifting cultivation. In the subsequent years, Bairagarh (1866) and Gugamal (1876) forests were declared as reserved forests. These forests were worked under Bagshaw's Working Plan (1893-1915). At the same time there were two working schemes, *viz.*, Gugamal Reserve Working Scheme (1910-1915) and Tapti Reserve Working Scheme (1912-1915). By 1913, the indiscriminate felling by the local tribes had been brought under control. Following this the area was worked for 20 years under improvement felling (Dunbar Brander's Working Plan, 1915-16 to 1935-36). Subsequently, these forests were worked for 20 years under uniform system in the better quality teak forests and "Coppice-with-Reserve" (CWR) in comparatively poorer quality forests (Stein's Plan, 1935-1955); and for another 15 years up to 1970, under "Selection-cum-Improvement" (SCI) felling in better quality teak forests and CWR in relatively poorer forests (Sharma's Plan, 1956-1970). Joshi's Working Plan (1975-1985) prescribed a separate working circle for wildlife with the objectives of "maintenance of viable wildlife populations" and "preservation of biologically important areas as national heritage".

In 1972, about 1600 km² of the Melghat forests were declared as a Tiger Reserve, which were later given the status of Melghat Wildlife Sanctuary in 1985. In 1987, a part of this sanctuary was declared as the Gugamal National Park. As a result of these changes, the first Management Plan for Melghat Tiger Reserve was written by Sheikh and Sawarkar, covering a period of 5 years (1973-74 to 1978-79). No regular long-term management plan was however written until 1987-88. This plan was written by Gogate (1988) for a 10 year period (1988-1998). Successive management plans have been written since then. In 1994, the boundary of Melghat Tiger Sanctuary was proposed to be redefined, excluding 551 km² with 39 villages from the sanctuary to form the proposed multiple-use zone, as it was not possible to relocate the villages within the sanctuary. At the same time 104 km² with 3 villages were to be added to the southern part of the reserve.

Bori forests are the oldest reserved forests (1865) in the country. Before the British took over the control of these forests in 1859, they were under the ownership of a *Korku* tribal chief, Bhupat Singh, These forests have enjoyed a long history of systematic management since 1897, with systematic fire protection introduced in 1884. The first working plan (Fernandez, 1897-1908) prescribed working the forests under improvement felling, so as to overcome the impact of decades of shifting cultivation. From 1909-1919, these forests were under Brander's plan, which continued with the Improvement Cycle. However, it was for the first time during this period, that accurate stock mapping was done. Improvement Felling Cycle was continued for another ten years, followed by Sodhi's plan (1928-1938), which prescribed conversion to uniform system and introduced an 80-years rotation. Under this working plan, 3 working circles were constituted, *viz.*, Bori Special Teak, High Forest and Low Forest. This continued under Macdonald's plan (1938-1947). With the commencement of Second World War however heavy felling was undertaken in these forests.

Thereafter, conversion period was increased to 120 years under Kulkarni's plan (1948-1963). This was continued under Jangley's plan (1965-1979) which was extended up to 1985. Some of the areas which were not fit for regeneration were worked under SCI. Mixed forests were put under improvement felling circle with 40-years cycle. In 1975, an area of 1427 km² in northern *Satpuras* was notified as Bori Sanctuary. In 1977, Pachmarhi Sanctuary was carved out of this to facilitate intensive management. Later in 1981 an area of 524 km² was taken from these two protected areas to form the Satpura National Park. The last working plan for Bori sanctuary was written by Gangopadhyay for the period 1986 to 1995. It prescribed the continuation of conversion to uniform system and changing from Improvement Felling to CWR system. It was for the first time however, that wildlife and its conservation was taken into consideration in a working plan. Consequently, care was taken to retain snags and fruit bearing trees. Moreover, all working in the area was stopped in 1991.

Geographic location

Melghat Tiger Reserve in Maharashtra and Bori Wildlife Sanctuary in Madhya Pradesh are situated in the Satpura hills within the 'Central Highlands' province of the Deccan Biogeographic Zone of Peninsular India (Rodgers and Panwar, 1988). The Satpuras are a range of hills which run from east to west along the boundary between Madhya Pradesh and Maharashtra. The most easterly branch of this range is called the Mykal, the centre as the Mahadeo and the western the Satpuras.

Melghat Tiger Reserve (1597 km²) in the southern Satpuras, is located in Dharni and Chikhalda Tahsils of Amravati district of Maharashtra (21° 15′ N to 21° 45′ N latitude and 76° 57′ E to 77° 30′ E longitude) about 50 km from Parathwada. The Tiger Reserve comprises the Melghat Wildlife Sanctuary (1315.65 km²) and the Gugamal National Park (361.28 km²). It is bounded on three sides by the forests of the East, West and South Melghat Divisions and river Tapti in the north and Betul district of Madhya Pradesh in the north and north-east.

Bori wildlife sanctuary (486 km²) is located in the south-eastern portion of Hoshangabad district of Madhya Pradesh state approximately 50 km from Itarsi. It falls in the Hoshangabad Forest Division, south of the Narmada river (22° 19′ N to 22° 30′ N latitude and 77° 56′ E to 78° 20′ E longitude). The sanctuary is situated in the midst of a large forest tract with the Satpura National Park in the north, Pachmarhi wildlife sanctuary, and forests of Hoshangabad and Chindwara divisions in the east and south-east, and forests of Betul division in the south, extending to the forests of Melghat and western Satpuras.

Physiographic characteristics and climate

Melghat Tiger Reserve consists of a succession of hills and valleys, marked by abrupt variations in altitude, aspect and gradient. It lies to the north of the Gawilgarh ridge, with numerous spurs branching off from this ridge within the reserve. These ridges have flat tops known as '*ballas*' and abrupt scarped sides forming narrow valleys below known as '*khoras*'. The southern part of the reserve is more rugged compared to the rest of the region. The area is drained by a number of streams in addition to 5 major rivers *viz.*, Khandu, Khapra, Sipna, Garga and Dolar, which form the tributaries of river Tapti. The drainage is towards north and north-west of the reserve. The highest point of Melghat region is at Bairat at 1178 m above MSL. The area of the reserve gradually descends towards the north-west about 950 m above MSL in the east and to about 381 m above MSL in the west, near river Tapti.

The formation of Melghat region is the Deccan trap, with lava flows found in a horizontal position. The underlying rock is basalt, in several forms, chiefly due to difference in the successive lava flows. The most common form is a hard dark coloured rock compact or fine grained. It occurs in thick layers and its outcrops give rise to scarps on hill sides. At times it is also found in river and stream beds, in the form of columns. The second form occurs in the lower hills; it is grey vesicular of amygdaloidal basalt, with crystals of quartz and other minerals, lining its cavities. The third is the basalt tuff, which is found in thin layers and is a soft grey, fine grained rock. The soil although fertile is generally stony as it is derived from the weathering and disintegration of underlying rock. Its depth and drainage vary considerably, from greater depth on lower slopes and valleys to very shallow on the steep upper slopes. There are three major soil types found in the region: 'Bouldery soil', which is most common throughout the reserve, is shallow and found on slopes, and is excessively drained resulting in loss of moisture during dry season; 'Clayey soil' which is very fertile, is found in low lying areas, however, it does not drain well; 'Lateritic loam' which is very shallow and dry is found on hill tops and plateaus.

Bori wildlife Sanctuary lies in undulating terrain, with the general slope being from East to West. While the north and north-eastern part is more rugged it more or less flattens out towards the west. The altitude in the sanctuary ranges from 305 m to 1045 m above MSL, with the highest point at Belkandhar peak, near Rorighat. The entire area is crisscrossed by perennial and annual streams and rivers. It also forms the catchment of the river Narmada, with tributaries like Malini, Koti, Bori, Sonbhadra and Tawa.

Rocks of Bori region belong to upper and lower Gondwana series. In the Bori area these consist of sandstones and abundant Deccan trap intrusions besides sandy shales, phyllite and schists, closely associated with limestone, are widely scattered. Extensive sandstones, with locally present clay represent the Damuda series. While Bagra and Denwa conglomerates occur in the middle reaches, Deccan trap with numerous dykes and sills is the major rock type in the lower reaches occurring in interspersion with alluvium along river banks. Soils are deep along the rivers, fairly deep and well drained on lower slopes and shallow on higher steep slopes.

In Melghat, the average temperature varies from a maximum of 43° C in summer to a minimum of 12° C in winter, with the higher hills and plateaus having a pleasant climate throughout the year. However while the valleys get very cold during the winter months (December to January), during summer, there is usually a marked difference in the day and night temperatures. Although the rainfall occurs during the rainy season from the middle of June to mid-October, occasional showers are experienced during December, January and March, with the annual rainfall varying from 1000 to 2250 mm. However, the rainfall is not well distributed and wide variations occur with change in altitude and topography. Moreover, except for 3 to 4 months of monsoons, the rest of the year is dry. Although, dew formation takes place, especially during winter months, its contribution to available moisture is insignificant. Frost though not common in the area is not unknown and generally occurs in the valleys.

The hottest months in Bori are from May to June with temperatures varying from a maximum average of 40° C in summer to minimum average of 22° C in winter. January and February are the coldest months with a minimum average temperature of 8° C. While the pre-monsoon showers usually start by end of May, the heaviest rain comes in July and August, with occasional showers in winter. The annual rainfall varies between 1200 to 3200 mm, with relative humidity highest during July and August and lowest in April and May. The Bori valley, however, experiences heavy dew until March and therefore these forests remain green for a longer period than other Teak forests in Madhya Pradesh.

Flora and fauna

While the forests of Melghat and Bori are dominated by teak, Melghat typically represents the Central Indian dry deciduous forest and Bori represents the South Indian moist deciduous forest. These forests are one of the oldest reserved forests in the country. Forests of Melghat belong to dry deciduous forest type of Central India, sub-group 5A of group 5 as per the classification given by Champion and Seth (1968). While teak is the dominant species (over 50%), depending upon altitude, gradient and other physiographic features, its associates may differ (Dhore and Joshi, 1988). While the most common teak associates in almost all localities are *Lagerstroemia parviflora, Lannea coromandelica, Emblica officinalis, Terminalia tomentosa, Anogeussus latifolia* and *Ougenia oojeinensis*; at lower elevations its associates are *Boswellia serrata, Wrightia tinctora, Acacia chundra, Cassia fistula, Miliusa tomentosa, Bauhinia racemosa* and *Butea monosperma*; and at higher elevations and in moist localities its associates are, *Mitragyna parviflora, Adina cordifolia, Schleichera oleosa, Albissia procera, Casearea elliptica*. The "Flora of Melghat Tiger Reserve" (Dhore and Joshi, 1988) documents 650 naturalised plant species, out of which 90 are tree species, 66 shrubs, 316 herbs, 56 climbers, 23 sedges and 99 grass species. In addition to these there are 72 cultivated species. The Research wing of the Tiger Reserve has also set up about 60 permanent vegetation plots to monitor floristic changes in response to rigid protection and habitat manipulation practices. Plantations were raised in the area under different plantation schemes and development activities.

While teak (*Tectona grandis*) is the dominant species, the major forest type in Bori is 3B, South Indian Moist Deciduous Forest (Champion and Seth, 1968), consisting of six different communities, *viz.*, moist miscellaneous forest at higher altitudes and in sheltered depressions, characterised by *Mangifera indica, Syzygium cuminii, Terminalia chebula* and *Ficus* species; mixed forest on gentler slopes along foothills, with *Terminalia tomentosa* and *Anogeissus latifolia*; low quality mixed forest in areas with sandstone as the underlying rock, characterised by *Chloroxylon swietenia, Pterocarpus marsupium* and *Lannea grandis*; good quality teak forest widely occurring in areas with soils derived from the trap, having a high percentage of teak with bamboo as understorey; low quality teak forest occurs in areas with drier trap soils and have an undergrowth of *Lantana* and *Petalidium*; and alluvial teak along river banks, characterised by really tall and well-formed stems. Another category is that of *Shorea robusta* mixed forest which grows on the adjoining Pachmarhi plateau and extends down on westerly slopes to integrate with the teak growing in Bori valley however it does not extend into the Bori forest. A floristic survey conducted in the area by State Forest Research Institute (SFRI), Jabalpur, identified as many as 1381 species belonging to different categories.

The forests of Central Indian highlands have been historically renowned for tiger, gaur and sambar, the latter two reaching their best form in this part of the country (Forsyth, 1889). Both Melghat Tiger Reserve and Bori Wildlife Sanctuary are rich in wild fauna, major species being the tiger, leopard, wild dog, hyena, jackal, sloth bear, *gaur, sambar,* barking deer, spotted deer, *chausingha, nilgai,* wild boar, along with more than 250 bird species, 21 species of reptiles, 24 species of fishes and 4 amphibians (Management Plans of Melghat and Bori). Although in Melghat animals like ratel, flying squirrel, python, pangolin and mouse deer are present they are not common. Regular tiger census and block and water hole counts are carried out annually in Melghat Tiger Reserve for monitoring densities of wild animals. Bori forests are inhabited by 14 endangered species of mammals, birds and reptiles. The flying squirrel (*Petaurista petaurista*), the Indian giant squirrel (*Ratufa indica*) and the mouse deer (*Tragulus meminna*) are one of the most sensitive to habitat changes (Sawarkar and Panwar, 1987).

Both Melghat and Bori have environmental and derived values, in terms of soil conservation and maintaining water regimes (Sawarkar and Panwar, 1987), as well as the floral and faunal diversity which provides sustenance and livelihood to the people who depend on them.

Chapter 4

Local Communities, Livelihoods and Forests

The problem of dependence of local communities on the resources of protected areas is much more complex than it appears to be. Deforestation, which may be the consequence of several factors, leads to environmental degradation and also causes economic hardship to local communities who depend on the forests (Thapa and Weber, 1990). However, deforestation itself is the result of more than one factor. Increasing landlessness and marginalisation of the local communities, lack of- employment opportunities in non-agriculture sector and support facilities in agricultural sector are considered to be the micro-level factors which force people to encroach on forest lands and increase the number of livestock (Bajracharya, 1983; Blaikie, 1985; Thapa and Weber, 1990). At the macro level however, it is the combined effect of growing human population, urbanisation, industrialisation and the emergence of the global economy, which has resulted in the exploitation of local agro-ecosystems by distant markets, especially of the developed world (McNeely, 1990; Thapa and Weber, 1990).

In the developing countries although one is tempted to lay the blame for the destruction of forests at the doorsteps of the local indigenous communities (Murthy, 1999), the actual causes of destruction however, remain obscure. This fallacy arises when the visible symptoms of the ailment (poaching, encroachment, etc.) conceal the causes *viz.*, unemployment, marginalisation, poverty and lack of alternatives, etc. (McNeely, 1990). While economic development is an important variable that can influence threats to protected areas, underdevelopment can lead to threats like poaching, timber smuggling etc., in the absence of alternative sources of employment and income (Machlis and Tichnell, 1987).

Thus conservation of biodiversity on long-term basis is possible only when local communities, who are an integral part of the ecosystem, are involved in protected area management. Moreover, the needs of these local communities should be taken care of by providing them alternative sources of income, energy and biomass so as to reduce their dependence on forest. It is also necessary to review our conservation and development policies in the light of the present socio-economic scenario. Such approach towards biodiversity conservation would require a detailed understanding of causes, magnitude and impact of people's dependence on protected areas.

Socio-economic data – collection and analysis

Classification of community groups

In earlier anthropological studies "methods of securing of food" have been used for the classification of societies into broad categories, e.g., food gatherers, hunters and fishers; pastoralists; agriculturists; and artisans (Firth 1956). For the purpose of this study however, different communities living in MTR and BWLS have been classified into three major categories depending on their social group and lifestyle. While 'social group' may be defined as tribal, backward or scheduled caste and others; 'lifestyle' may be defined as the way of living and earning livelihood, values, practices and activities (Park and Park, 1991). For this study, the activities and practices of each social group were taken into consideration to define 'lifestyle'.

Scheduled tribes

These people were culturally and ethnically distinct, but over the years they have adopted the ways of the mainstream contemporary urban Indian society through the process of acculturation. All the major tribal communities studied, i.e., *Korku, Gond, Nehal, Burad* (*Basor*) and *Rathiya* have been grouped in this category. The *Korku, Gond, Nehal* (considered an offshoot of the *Korku* tribe) had been original hunters and shifting cultivators before the British took over these forests. The *Burad / Basor* tribe were original bamboo basket makers. The British encouraged the tribal communities living in these forests to settle down in villages so that they could provide labour for the timber extraction activities. Consequently, since the beginning of forestry operations in this region, these tribes have been involved in logging and related forestry activities as labourers. Earnings from employment in forestry sector have formed a major source of income for these people. The *Rathiya* tribe however, had settled in the Melghat region comparatively more recently. They were originally from Madhya Pradesh and had come to

Melghat as labourers. Most of these families were landless
however they took land on rent for growing cash crops.
Agriculture was primarily for subsistence although some
landholders especially in MTR were engaged in a limited
amount of cash cropping.

Scheduled and backward classes

The other major community group was a large mix
of various scheduled and backward classes, who were
engaged in agriculture in addition to being employed in
jobs or being engaged in commercial activities. *Balais*
who formed majority of this group were originally
weavers (*Bunkars*). *Balai, Vanjaris, Lohars* and *Gaolan*
were grouped under this category, as these people were
generally practising agriculture, but had also taken up
various jobs and professions over the years due to facilities
and concessions provided to them.

Agro-pastoralists

The third major community group comprised of cowherds,
milkmen and cattle-breeders, i.e., *Gawli*. Their lifestyle
was agro-pastoralist in nature. Originally the agro-
pastoralists did not belong to these areas, but over the years
had migrated into these forests from adjoining regions due
to increasing population pressure and depleting resources.

Data were collected from both primary and secondary
sources and analysed to assess the socio-economic status
and dependence of both tribal and non-tribal communities
in Melghat Tiger Reserve and Bori Wildlife Sanctuary.
Primary data were collected through household interviews,
surveys and group discussions while secondary data on

the villages within the two PAs were collected from the respective District and Forest Departments. While village records were available with the revenue department in Melghat, the office of the Project Tiger, Melghat had also collected demographic data on the villages under its eco-development program. However, the data for the villages within Bori Wildlife Sanctuary were available only with the Forest Department as these were forest villages. The past records for these villages were however, not available.

Both qualitative and quantitative methods were used for data collection. Informal meetings and group discussions with the villagers were arranged to make them aware of the objectives of the survey and the probable outcome. Moreover, these were used to gather general information on the villages regarding the functioning of the civic bodies and problems faced by the villagers as well as to develop a seasonal calendar of activity for the people. Care was taken to record all information being given by the respondents during these interactions.

The group discussions were mostly held in the presence of the *Sarpanch* and / or *Patel*, whose house was generally used for the purpose. However, in their absence any respected village elder was invited to head the village meetings. Ideally a study of this nature could be carried out more successfully through the method of participant observation (Mayer, 1975). However this would have required more time than was available for the present study. Besides, during this study a large number of villages had to be surveyed and therefore, it was not possible to use the participant observation method. Instead, the author stayed in the village and carried out what is termed as non-participant observation or quasi-participant observation (Goode and Hatt, 1954) through informal group discussions which proved helpful in giving time both to the author and the respondents to develop a mutual trust and understanding.

In addition to the group discussions, questionnaire method was also used. Both open- and closed-ended questionnaires were designed to elicit response. Moreover, to allow easy interpretation and analysis, fixed response questions were also included. The questionnaire was designed and pretested in the field during the reconnaissance. During the household surveys, effort was made to reduce any gender or generation bias by interviewing all the adult members in the family together. Moreover, during the household interviews, a person from each village accompanied the author in addition to a local assistant. This helped to cross-check the information given by the respondents, and to interpret the local languages (*Korku, Gondi, Marathi*), whenever used. The information obtained during the interviews and discussions was further corroborated with the information obtained through observations made by the author during her stay in each of the sample villages.

The household interviews were used to collect data on both demographic parameters and dependence on the forest. The demographic data included demographic structure (information on family size, age and sex of the family members), number of people in working age group (18 to 60 years), division of labour, level of literacy, occupation, the size of landholding, livestock holding (milk and draught animals) and crops grown. To assess people's dependence on the forest, information was collected from each household on the resources extracted from the forest every year. Data were collected on quantity of fuel wood, timber and types of non-timber forest produce (NTFP) collected, quantities consumed and sold each year and contribution to the annual income of the family.

Data were analysed separately for different communities and comparisons were carried out across the communities both within each of the PAs as well as across the two PAs. Data were collected to determine social status of the households on the basis of land and livestock ownership, number of people employed in - jobs, business, or as labourer, number of days in an year for which labour employment was available and income earned from these sources.

Sample villages had to be selected from both MTR and BWLS and were classified as large, medium and small, using the available secondary information. Villages were stratified on the basis of human and livestock populations. Sample villages were selected from each strata taking care to include villages with both homogenous and heterogeneous population composition so as to cover the major communities, both tribal and non-tribal, living in these protected areas. Simple random sampling was followed for the household surveys in the selected villages. Every third household was sampled. In case the members of the selected household were not present or not willing to respond, the next third household was selected. It was not possible to select households in advance, and the author had to depend on the ground situation in field, in terms of availability of the respondents and their willingness to respond. Consequently, the sample size varied from village to village. To overcome this problem, all the sampled households were pooled together for each study area. From this pooled sample the households were then put into their respective community groups. More than 20% of the villages and households were sampled in both MTR and BWLS. While 243 families (out of 901 in 15 villages) were sampled in MTR, 75 families (out of 204 in 5 villages) were sampled in BWLS.

Socio-economic data were analysed so as to determine the relationship between various community groups in Melghat and Bori.

Fuel wood and timber

Households in both MTR and BWLS used fuel wood for cooking food and heating water as well as for keeping houses warm during monsoon and winter months. The wood used by the local people for cooking and heating purposes, as well as timber (collected from the forest) for the houses, fences, etc. was extracted from the forest around the villages. Fuel wood was collected daily from the forest and carried in the form of head-loads by the people. As the respondents were not able to specify the fuel wood consumption for cooking purposes in terms of head-loads and moreover, a high variability was found in the responses about weight of a head-load. Thus, it was necessary to standardise the head-load weight, per capita consumption of fuel wood for cooking purposes and per household requirement of fuel wood for heating the houses. Households belonging to different community groups and socio-economic strata were selected for the purpose. Thus, head-loads were weighed in 30 households and a mean head-load weight (17.71kg. ± 0.76) was calculated. To standardise daily fuel wood consumption for cooking purposes, 26 families from different community groups and villages were monitored for 4 days (1.28 kg ± 0.83

for the tribal; and 1.58 kg ± 1.48 for the agro-pastoralist). For calculating the per capita fuel wood consumption for cooking purposes, the adult units per family were calculated based on the following conversion scale (Mishra and Ramakrishnan, 1982): Adult man = 1 unit; Adult woman = 0.9 units; Child = 0.7 units. The total number of adult units (AU) in a family were calculated as:

$$AU = (1 \times M) + (0.9 \times F) + (0.7 \times C); \text{ where,}$$

M = Number of adult men; F = Number of adult women; C = Number of children.

Per capita fuel wood consumption was calculated as: PF = DF / AU, where,

PF = Daily per capita fuel wood consumption; DF = Daily fuel wood consumption per household; AU = Total adult units in a family; and

$$AF = PF \times N \text{ where,}$$

AF = Annual per capita fuel wood consumption; PF = Daily per capita fuel wood consumption; N = 365 (Number of days in a year).

The fuel wood consumption for heating the houses during monsoon and winter months (July to March = 9 months) was calculated separately for each family by weighing the wood in 30 families in Melghat during winter. The procedure was similar to that followed for measuring the head-loads in households. Thus a mean quantity of wood required for heating purposes per household was calculated as follows:

AW = W×N, where,

AW = Quantity of wood consumed annually per household;
W = Quantity of wood consumed per family per day; N =
Number of days = 270 (i.e., 9 months×30 days).

Thus, the total fuel wood consumption in the area was
calculated by adding up the total wood consumed both
for cooking and heating purposes. The limitation of this
method is that the quantity calculated will not be accurate
since the wood consumption will vary with the quality
and type of wood available and used by the people.

Households were also asked about their timber
requirements, various types of timber required and the
purposes for which it was required. Although people were
able to give information regarding the different types
of timber required and the purposes for which it was
required, they were not very sure of the amount required
by them for the various purposes *viz.*, house construction
and repairs, fencing and agricultural implements and
other household articles.

Non-timber forest produce and agriculture

Information on various NTFPs collected by the villagers,
the season of collection, various crops grown and
agricultural activity-pattern, was gathered during group
discussions. This information was used to chalk out a
calendar of seasonal activities.

Moreover, each household was asked to recall the various
NTFP items collected by them from the forest during the
past one year and also to specify the quantities collected

/ sold / or consumed. It was found that if the item was a marketable product it was easier for the respondents to remember the quantity collected and sold. However, for items which were mostly collected for domestic consumption, (especially forest vegetables, mushrooms, tubers, fishes, crabs, grasses and leaves for fodder and thatching), the respondents were unable to give the exact quantity. In such cases they gave approximations in terms of 'basketfuls', 'handfuls', or number of meals or days the item was eaten. The respondents also found it difficult to recall quantities of grasses or leaves collected for fodder or thatching in the past one year and therefore these items were left out of the quantification.

For the purpose of analysis the NTFP items have been grouped into major categories of flowers, seeds and fruits, mushrooms, bamboo shoots, roots and tubers, forest vegetables, fishes and crabs. The money value of the items that were marketed by the sample households was directly calculated. The non-marketed items like mushrooms, bamboo shoots, roots and tubers, etc., were not considered for quantification.

Each household was also asked to specify the crops grown in the past one year, and to assess the amount of damage to crop in terms of percentage of the total, the quantity produced and sold and the earnings from it. In Melghat, the villagers were able to give approximate quantity of crop produced as majority of them were selling part of the agriculture produce either in the local markets or in nearby towns. The households in Bori sanctuary were however, unable to specify the quantity produced or sold as they were not selling the agricultural produce. However, they could give approximate damage to the crop due to various factors like excess or scarcity of water, insects and other pests and disease. Therefore, income from agriculture and the value of agricultural produce could be calculated for the households in Melghat only.

Income

While data on income from agriculture (not available for BWLS), dairy activities, sale of NTFPs and fuel wood, employment / trade / enterprise, were given by the respondents, income from labour activities had to be calculated by the author as it was not a regular source. For this purpose data were collected from each household for the number of days labour employment was available to a person in a year and this was used to calculate the mean number of days in a year for which employment was available to a person. As no standardised formula was available for calculating household earnings from labour activities, it was developed by for this study by the author. Annual household earning from labour activities was calculated as follows:

$I_L = (M) \times (N) \times (W)$; where,

M = Mean number of employment days per person per year; N = Number of people in working age in a family; W = Daily wages per person (Indian Rupees at 1996 prices); I_L = Income per family per year from labour activities (Indian Rupees at 1996).

This method gives an approximation of the income earned from labour employment, as it depends on the availability of employment opportunities. Moreover, it assumes that all the members of a family in the working age group are getting employed for the mean number of days per month. The formula thus calculates the maximum income that may be earned by the family through labour activities. The total annual income of a family was calculated as:

$I = I_A + I_D + I_F + I_L + I_O$, where,

I = Total annual income of a family; I_A = Income from agriculture; I_D = Income from dairy activities; I_F = Income from sale of forest produce (NTFP); I_L = Income from labour activities (calculated); I_O = Income from any other sources (regular employment, business, sale of fuel wood, etc.). However, the total annual income of a family may be taken as an approximation of the actual income accruing to the family, as most of the sources except income from regular employment were highly variable.

Limitations

It was not possible to conduct a truly 'random' household survey because quite a few of the landless families migrate to the towns in search of employment opportunities and are therefore absent from the villages for major part of the year. This may have introduced a limited sampling bias. Moreover, some of the respondents viewed the author as being associated with the forest department and were therefore reluctant to be interviewed or divulge information (especially related to amounts of NTFPs and fuel wood collected). Also, people in some villages, who had been previously interviewed by other agencies, were sceptical about the utility of the exercise and were not willing to spend time or answer accurately. Although it was difficult to assess the response bias, the information collected through informal discussions and group meetings with the villagers showed that the results did reflect the local opinion.

This study however, was a major empirical study of the socio-economic scenario in both MTR and BWLS. In the absence of any other comparable secondary data on the relevant parameters, it was difficult to check the validity of all the information collected during the course of this study. Since this was a maiden attempt and moreover, field conditions were so variable, detailed investigations could not be carried out in the stipulated time.

Social organisation and structure

Several people oriented studies have been done e.g., Russell and Lal (1975) have done a detailed documentation of the tribes and castes of Central India, their religion, social customs, inheritance laws, etc. Fuchs (1988) in his study on the Korkus of Vindhya hills has also referred to various studies on Korkus of Melghat region. Apart from this many studies on family structure and change have been conducted to examine the impact of urbanisation and industrialisation in the rural and urban areas. It is however, worthwhile to note that few studies have directed their attention to structure and organisation of tribal families *per se*. The paucity of such literature has been pointed out by Shah (1996).

Both Melghat and Bori regions are mostly inhabited by tribes (80%), who with the establishment of British administration in the region in the 19th century were encouraged to give up shifting cultivation and settle down. *Korku* is the predominant tribe in the region. Melghat Tiger

Reserve has *Gond, Nehal, Thatia, Burad* and *Rathiya* tribes apart from the *Korkus*. Bori Wildlife Sanctuary however, has only *Korku, Gond* and *Thatia* tribes. The remaining 20% of the population in the two PAs is non-tribal, i.e., scheduled castes and other backward classes. Most of them belong to agro-pastoralist communities (15%), *viz., Gawli*. The remaining 5% belong to scheduled castes and other backward classes, majority of which are the *Balai, Vanjari* and *Lohar*. Bori Wildlife Sanctuary has only *Gawlis* in addition to the tribal community.

Various tribes and castes co-existing in MTR and BWLS displayed a basically patriarchal structure. Tribes and non-tribes mostly lived in nuclear family units. Within the community, in general, and the family in particular, the division of labour was traditional to a certain extent i.e., women were necessarily responsible for performing all the household chores like cooking, rearing and nurturing the children. Moreover, the tribal women also participated in agricultural activities and even worked as wage labourers. Non-tribal women especially of the agro-pastoral households also participated in various cattle rearing activities within the house. Moreover, it was women who were responsible for collecting fuel wood and non-timber forest produce from the forests.

Festivals like Holi and Diwali also were occasions when the young and the old as well as the men and the women joined in drinking *mahua* (country liquor made from the flower of *Madhuca latifolia*) and dancing and generally having a good time. Seeing them on such occasions it was difficult to visualise how a people so completely dependent on the forest for sustenance and living within limited means could exhibit such enthusiasm. It was probably in this manner that enthusiasm for life kept them smiling and prevented them from giving up their struggle for survival even in the worst of times. The solidarity of the tribal community is perhaps expressed through their dancing and drinking as has been observed by other anthropologists and sociologists like Durkheim (1976) and Radcliffe-Brown (1979).

Community structure and religion

Although majority of the population in both the PAs was predominantly tribal, other castes especially the *Gawlis* were also present, resulting in a heterogeneous population. Three major community groups (A, B and C) were therefore identified. Community A consisted of different scheduled tribes, community B mostly consisted of scheduled and backward classes and community C were agro-pastoralists. Each of these communities practised their own religion and considered proper performance of religious observances as a necessary part of their community life. As such religious actions were expected to obtain some specific benefit like health, long life, success in growing crops, bringing rain, multiplication of cattle, etc. Earlier studies have suggested that some tribes, especially the *Korkus* of the Central Indian Provinces consider themselves as Hindus, but like many other lower Hindu castes their religion is mostly purely *'Animistic'* (Russell and Lal, 1975). Among the tribes under study both *Animism* and *totemism* were practised. This was evident from the variety of trees in the forest which were sacredly draped with colourful cloth pieces for propitiation. Sometimes small worship places of stone or mud under the sacred trees were also found. These were perhaps the village deities which Russell and Lal

(1975) have referred to as *Mutua Deo*. Most of the fields too had mud or wooden totems erected outside the fields. Durkheim (1976) has also described the presence of such totems among Australian aborigines. He refers to them as sacred religious symbols. In the present study the totems mostly signified the family ancestors as described by the respondents. During sowing and harvesting seasons the totems were decorated and spruced up for propitiation. According to Durkheim (1976) and Radcliffe-Brown (1979) the propitiation of the totems helps the community in reiterating its solidarity. The non-tribals who practised Hindu religion either had a small portion of a wall in the house carved out particularly for prayers and it was often observed that women generally went in groups singing traditional holy songs and worshipped under some particular trees in the forest.

Family organisation

As far as the family profile was concerned various studies have defined a family as a residential family group which is called a household consisting of a couple living under the same roof with or without unmarried children. While a joint family may be defined as a commensal unit composed of two or more related married couples plus their unmarried children. It has also been suggested that substituting the term "extended family" to refer to residential joint family or the commensal joint family is also feasible (Kolenda, 1968). Other sociologists have considered a family as a joint family if it was eating from one *chulha* (hearth), sharing property and rights, pocket book, larder, debts, labour and usually one head (Cohn, 1961). Mayer (1960) has defined a household as those who "share a cooking hearth, pool their incomes and have living expenses in common".

According to the findings of the present study, nuclear families were predominant while there were very few joint and extended families. Shah (1964, 1968, 1973 and 1996) and Desai (1955) have also reported the existence of nuclear families in tribal and rural areas. There were also examples of quasi-joint families where the kitchen was separate even though they all stayed in the same compound. At times both or the surviving elderly parents were found to be living with one of the son's families and the father continued to be the head of this household and shared the common kitchen. Here also no definite pattern was found but most often it was the eldest son with whom the parents lived. In the majority of cases after marriage the son moved out of his parental home and built a small house for himself and his wife. While they lived as a separate household unit and were economically independent, they continued to share the agricultural land owned by his father although he did not have any inheritance rights on the land as has also been reported by Russell and Lal (1975) in their study. Thus, when a tribal had several sons each would be living in a neo-local unit, and yet he would continue to share his duties for cultivating the land with his paternal family.

All families were basically patriarchal in nature, with the father as the head of the family. There was a strict division of labour with women being assigned household chores and nurturing their children. They had however, no egalitarian role in the structure and were to some extent subservient to men with no authority in marital roles. Men were the main authoritative figures and all major decisions relating to family matters, code of behaviour and family expenditure were taken them. Besides, it was observed that the men were highly protective towards their women. This was indicated by the fact that all dealings with outsiders regardless of gender were done by men. The women themselves did not venture to face outsiders (when the author went to do her field work in the first round, it was usually the men who participated in the group discussions and only after several visits to the village did the women openly talk to the author). This could be due to their socialisation or could have been a result of being specifically instructed by the elders. It is interesting to note that while the women carried the full burden of household duties from fetching water and fuel wood, cooking food, washing clothes and utensils and rearing the children, they were also expected to share the work on the family's agricultural fields. The women also worked as wage labourers to supplement the family income whenever required. The money thus earned however, became part of the family earnings over which the women had no control.

Certain differences in the family organisation were observed in the tribal families as compared to the non-tribal families. As far as the tribal community was concerned, despite the patriarchal nature, men and women exhibited a strong companionship. This was reflected in their various daily activities e.g., collection of NTFPs like *Mahua*, *tendu* and *chironji*, catching fish in the rivers and streams, taking the cattle for grazing in the forest, or even working together in harvesting or sowing seasons. All such activities called for the participation of the entire tribal household unit. Apart from this companionship the tribal women appeared to have greater freedom in matters concerning matrimony. This was also reflected at the time of spouse selection; both men and women had an equal say in the selection of their life partner.

Although monogamy was the common norm, rare incidence of polygamy (<1%) were also observed especially, in cases where the first wife was not able to bear children. However, in the observed cases both the wives were found to be living in the same house or close by, with the children of the second wife addressing the first wife as "*bari ma*" for mother. Men and women were allowed to form a common law marriage union as well. This was wholly acceptable in the tribal community. Moreover, the children born out of such marriages were also accepted. There were incidences where the woman had chosen her man, lived with him for some years or even bore his child before they finally formalised the marriage relationship. The woman also had the freedom to change or leave her husband for another man; she only had to inform the family and the elders of the village about her decision. On the whole the tribal society appeared to be far more liberal than the non-tribal society.

As compared to the tribal community, the non-tribal (scheduled and backward classes and the agro-pastoralists) exhibited a different family organisation. Although in the non-tribal community, the same family structure as described above was the norm, i.e., the men were the major decision makers, the relationship between men and women however, was not as friendly as that observed in the tribal society. The pattern of division of labour within the household units was however, similar to the one existing in the tribal community. But other major differences were also observed especially in the pattern of spouse selection. More often than not a few marriages were arranged by proxy and mostly during childhood, even though cases of child marriage were not reported. Common law marriage was un-common and was not acceptable. Any pre-marital relationships between men and women were contemptuously labelled as "tribal".

Restrictions on women's employment were imposed by men, especially whenever the men were either employed in government organisations or were engaged in small business. In such families it was considered *infra dig* for women to take up wage labour employment. The women however, joined the men in all agricultural activities. They did not exhibit the same pattern of companionship as was seen among the tribal. In the agro-pastoralist households the women worked with the men in rearing the livestock as well as in all other dairy activities. The relationship between husband and wife in the non-tribal society was not one of companionship but rather one of subordination and super-ordination.

Socio-economic scenario

Out of the 61 revenue villages in Melghat Tiger Reserve, 6 were located on the periphery of Gugamal National Park, which was the core of the Tiger Reserve (Table 1). Although entry in the core was strictly prohibited, the people and livestock from these villages were dependent on the forest adjacent to the core. This resulted in management problems for the forest department and hardships to the people living in these villages. All the 17 villages in Bori Wildlife Sanctuary were forest villages (Table 1). Since it was decided to convert the status of the three PAs, i.e., Satpura NP, Bori and Pachmarhi sanctuaries to a Tiger Reserve, the process of public meetings and selection of suitable sites to relocate these villages outside the sanctuary was carried out. Human population density in both MTR ($19.15/km^2$) and BWLS ($8.23/km^2$) was lower than India's population density (all India figures of human population density were $286.9/km^2$; World Resources Institute, 1992). While livestock density for MTR was $20.14/km^2$, for BWLS it was $15.43/km^2$.

Most of the villages were heterogeneous in nature, with different communities living together. The basic outlay of the villages was very similar, with a straight lane in the middle and the houses lined on either side of it, opening on to the lane. Larger villages had several rows of houses in parallel lanes. The houses were usually built of timber and bamboo poles, with mud covered bamboo matting used as walls. The roofs were slanting and covered with locally made baked mud tiles. There was sometimes a raised platform in front of some of the houses, used for sitting outside. Some of the houses had a long narrow veranda in front or at the back of the house. The doors were placed in the front and back walls of the houses and were very low, with the roof projecting above it. Depending on the size and economic status of the family, the houses had one or more parallel rooms or sections, with one leading into another and a door in the back wall which opened in the rear of the house. While a part of the main room was used as kitchen and for storing agricultural and forest produce in large mud urns fixed on the floor, the rest of the room may be used for sleeping, etc. The interiors of the houses were usually very dark and without proper ventilation, except for the front and back doors, windows were conspicuously absent.

Table 1: Basic socio-economic information of the villages in Melghat Tiger Reserve and Bori Wildlife Sanctuary

Parameters	MTR	BWLS
Number of villages	61	17
Type of villages	Revenue	Forest
Area under cultivation* (km²)	109.84	37.34
*As percentage of the total area	8.34%	7.68%
Human population	25196	4000
Livestock population	26499	7500
Villages included in sampling	15 (24.5)	5 (29.4)
Households sampled	243 (22.9)	75 (37.5)
Population sampled	1616 (26.4)	485 (35.4)
Tribal households	167 (69.0)	64 (85.0)
Non-tribal households	76 (31.0)	11 (15.0)
Landholders	168 (69)	69 (92)
Livestock holders	210 (86.4)	67 (89.3)

Source: Records of the revenue department (Maharashtra) and forest departments of Melghat Tiger Reserve and Bori Wildlife Sanctuary (1996). *Figures in parentheses are percentages of the total of each parameter. MTR=Melghat Tiger Reserve; BWLS=Bori Wildlife Sanctuary.*

The backyard usually had a small kitchen garden called the *'baari'*, where maize and vegetables were grown. In addition to this there was usually a small bamboo enclosure for bathing and washing. Toilets were conspicuous by their absence and people went to the forest or agricultural fields. However, just as the author had completed her study in MTR, the government scheme of setting up subsidised toilets in people's houses for recycling bio-waste had been initiated. The initial response seemed encouraging; work had already begun in a few houses scattered over several villages (e.g. Jarida, Semadoh).

The livestock was usually tied in front of the houses. The agro-pastoralists however, constructed cattle sheds adjacent to or in front of their houses for keeping their large herds of cattle during the night. The sheds were made of thick wooden and bamboo poles, with the roofs covered with leaves for shade and were also used for storing cut grasses and cattle feed. While the agricultural fields were away from the houses, and usually close to natural water source if any. The vegetable garden (*baari*) was located adjoining to the houses. The agricultural fields and the '*baaris*' were fenced using bamboo and wooden poles or lantana and other thorny material from the forest. The fields had a raised wooden platform, called a '*manda*', in the middle for keeping a watch on the fields, especially during the nights.

As far as the village administration was concerned, the *patel* and the *sarpanch* were the local heads, who exercised varying control on the villages under their jurisdiction. They were responsible for settling local issues and disputes and were also the village representatives. Apart from this they did not seem to have any role in controlling natural resource-use by the local people. In addition to these local heads, villages in MTR also had *gram-sevaks,* who were grass root level workers of the revenue department, as these villages were under the preview of the latter. Each *gram-sevak* looked after several villages and formed a link between the people and the Block Development officer. He was also responsible for maintaining records of the revenue department, pertaining to human and livestock populations, size and ownership of landholding, land deeds and all related matters.

The villages however, lacked most of the basic civic amenities like proper drinking water, electricity, roads, dispensaries, toilets, etc. Each village had one or two hand pumps depending on the size of the village, but most of them were found out of order. In MTR, some of the villages had one or two water taps, for providing running water. The water situation was quite bad, especially in the remote villages where there were neither hand pumps nor wells and the villagers had to walk up to a kilometre in the forest to wells or *nallahs* (streams or rivulets) to fetch their daily requirement of water. The livestock too had to be taken to these water sources twice a day, especially during summers.

As far as electricity supply was concerned, while quite a few villages in MTR had regular electricity supply, none of the villages in BWLS had this facility although some of the villages had solar street lights. However, solar lights and lanterns did not seem to have been successful, due to poor maintenance. Moreover, during the monsoon months due to cloudy weather, these could not get recharged regularly. Consequently, most of the villages were without light after sunset.

Apart from the local existing economic system the influence of modern banking was observed in some villages. For example, MTR had a moderately fair network of nationalised banks like the State Bank of India and the Allahabad Bank. The villagers had also been given loans under various bank schemes. Some of the villages had regular postal service. In addition to a road network connecting all the villages especially in fair weather, two state highways cut across MTR. There were regular state and inter-state bus services available for the villagers in MTR. These banking and postal services as well as state transport were completely missing in BWLS. As far as communication was concerned MTR was well connected by a wireless network. In the Bori sanctuary however, they had only recently been installed in a few places.

Like the modern banking system, which had made inroads in some areas, the modern education system had also become an integral part of the village structure. Both MTR and BWLS had several day and boarding (called *Ashram*) schools run by government and private agencies (in MTR). Despite the facilities provided for school education, most of the children from tribal households lacked the motivation for attending regular school. Consequently, illiteracy amongst the tribal population was high, both in MTR and BWLS. Even the school drop-out rate for this community group was high (more than 50%) at primary and secondary levels. Moreover, in MTR most of the children from backward and scheduled classes were found to be attending regular school. In BWLS however, girls from *Gawli* households were found attending regular school.

The health facilities were comparatively better in MTR, especially in villages connected by tar roads, with primary health centres (PHCs) and mobile medical squads which made weekly visits to the remote villages once a week. In addition to this, there were nurses posted in the villages looking after 4-5 villages. Moreover, more than 50% of families in MTR were covered under Family Planning Scheme. In BWLS these facilities were almost non-existent, with the government nurses mostly absent from the villages due to lack of supervision and inadequate medicine stocks supplied to them for treating the patients.

As far as veterinary services were concerned, there were veterinary hospitals in and around MTR, and people were found seeking medical help for their livestock. However, the scenario in BWLS was quite bad. Although the animal husbandry department made annual visits to the villages for immunising the livestock it did not receive people's participation or co-operation.

Socio-economic profile and demographic characteristics

More than 75% of the households and population sampled across the two PAs belonged to community A, which comprised of the tribal community. The remaining households belonged to communities B and C, i.e., the non-tribal (Table 2). Data collected in household surveys was used to calculate the mean family size, mean number of adult males, females and children and mean number of adult units per family. The mean family size was slightly lower in BWLS (6.45 ±0.31) as compared to MTR (6.65 ±0.81.81). While the number of adult males (BWLS: 1.65 ±0.10; MTR: 1.93 ±0.07) and adult females (BWLS: 1.81 ±0.10; MTR: 1.82 ±0.06) per household was found to be higher in MTR, the mean number of children per household was higher for BWLS (2.99 ±0.23) than for MTR (2.93 ±0.13). However, number of adult units was higher for MTR (5.61 ±0.15) as compared to BWLS (5.39 ±0.25).

Azra Musavi

Table 2: Family size and demographic parameters of sample households in Melghat Tiger Reserve and Bori Wildlife Sanctuary

Area	MTR			BWLS	
Communities	A	B	C	A	C
No. of families*	167 (53)	48 (15)	28 (9)	64 (20)	11 (3)
Population*	1138 (54.2)	301 (14.3)	178 (8.5)	414 (19.7)	70 (3.3)
Family size**	6.81 (0.22)	6.25 (0.42)	6.36 (0.54)	6.47 (0.35)	6.36 (0.66)
Adult males / family**	1.95 (0.09)	1.94 (0.16)	1.89 (0.21)	1.67 (0.12)	1.55 (0.21)
Adult females / family**	1.79 (0.07)	1.90 (0.13)	1.86 (0.25)	1.73 (0.09)	2.27 (0.38)
Children / family**	3.09 (0.16)	2.54 (0.32)	2.61 (0.33)	3.06 (0.26)	2.55 (0.45)
Adult units / family**	5.71 (0.18)	5.38 (0.33)	5.47 (0.51)	5.39 (0.28)	5.37 (0.56)
Working age members / family**	3.37 (0.12)	3.42 (0.26)	3.32 (0.35)	3.05 (0.17)	3.73 (0.59)

*Figures in parentheses are percentages. **Mean value (Standard Error).*

MTR=Melghat Tiger Reserve; BWLS=Bori Wildlife Sanctuary;

A=Scheduled Tribes; B=Scheduled Castes and Backward Classes; and C=Agro-pastoralists.

Family size and demographic parameters for different communities across the two PAs were also calculated. However Kruskal-Wallis one-way ANOVA did not show any significant differences for either of the parameters. Mean family size was more or less similar across the two PAs. The mean number of adult males per family was highest for communities A and B in MTR however the mean number of adult females was highest for community C in BWLS. Although mean number of children per family was high for community A in both PAs, mean number of members in working age was more or less similar for all communities across the two PAs. The adult units per family were also similar (Table 2).

It was observed that in landholding families other than agro-pastoral communities i.e., A and B, all the family members, whether living together or separately participated in common agricultural activities except in the cases of land dispute within the family. The old members and the children however, were usually exempted from these duties. The produce too was distributed amongst the members according to their due share. For the agro-pastoralists too, cattle rearing and its related activities were more or less a family activity, where the men and young boys accompanied the cattle to forest and milked the cattle; it was the women who did the processing of the milk and other dairy jobs. However, while mostly the men went to sell milk and dairy products, in some cases women and even young boys were found doing this work. As far as the unemployed and landless families (across all communities) were concerned, depending on the availability of labour employment opportunities, work was taken up by all those in the working age group.

Apart from helping in the agricultural fields, cattle rearing and dairy activities and doing labour work, the women were mostly found to be responsible for fetching drinking water, collecting fuel wood, fodder, NTFP and thatching grasses and cooking food, for the family apart from all other domestic chores. The men on the other hand were responsible for agricultural jobs, repairing their houses, grazing cattle and selling NTFPs and agricultural surplus.

Land and livestock ownership

Land and livestock ownership across different communities in the two PAs was examined. More than 60 per cent of the families had both land and livestock, whereas only 8 per cent had neither land nor livestock. While 6 per cent families owned only land, 18 per cent owned only livestock. It was found that 70 per cent of the non-agro-pastoralists in Melghat and Bori and the agro-pastoralists in Bori had both land and livestock. However, 64 per cent of agro-pastoralists in MTR had only livestock. Eight per cent of non-agro-pastoralists in MTR and BWLS were without land or livestock (Figure 1).

Agriculture and landholding pattern

Agriculture in the region has historically been for sustenance. The local tribal community practised shifting cultivation until the late 18th and early 19th century, when the British persuaded them to give up this practice and adopt a settled lifestyle. This was in the interest of the British government, which needed labour for their timber logging operations in the Satpura forests. Population growth over the years had resulted in the agricultural land being fragmented into smaller and smaller landholding, especially where families had divided into separate households. Most of the landholdings were marginal or small. As a result agriculture in most of the cases was only for subsistence. In addition to this, most of the families were landless.

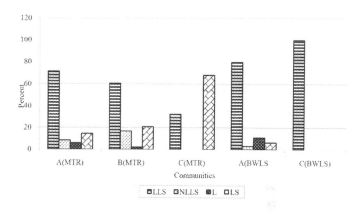

LLS=Land & livestock; NLLS=No land & livestock; L=Land only; LS=Livestock only.

Fig. 1: Land and livestock ownership pattern across communities in Melghat Tiger Reserve (MTR) and Bori Wildlife Sanctuary (BWLS)

All landholders, irrespective of size of landholding, practised traditional agriculture using bullock drawn ploughs. Seeds were sown either manually or through a wooden funnel attached to a hollow bamboo pole fixed to the plough. All agricultural related activities of weeding, harvesting and winnowing were also done manually. Agriculture was rain fed and only the large landholders are able to hire diesel pumps for irrigating their fields. Fertilisers were mostly used by large landholders who had access to irrigation e.g., lift irrigation. The smaller holders did not have access to irrigation or credit and therefore rarely used chemical fertilisers. While the main monsoon crops were various indigenous varieties of paddy, soya bean and pulses, the main winter crops were wheat, gram and *jagni* (oil seed).

However as mentioned above, agriculture being rain dependent, not many people were able to grow winter crops, except where the moisture was retained in the soil till the winter sowing season or the landholder had access and resources to irrigate his field. Some of the areas had black cotton soil, but due to lack of agricultural inputs and know-how, and inadequate irrigation facilities, the landholders were not able to exploit this potential.

Table 3: Landholding pattern of sampled households in Melghat Tiger Reserve and Bori Wildlife Sanctuary

Parameters	MTR	BWLS
Landholder households	168 (69)	69 (92)
Marginal & small landholders (≤5acres)	83 (49.5)	62 (89.9)
Medium & large landholders (>5 ares)	85 (50.5)	7 (10.1)
Landless households	75 (30.8)	6 (8)
Households renting land	18 (7.4)	2 (2.6)
Households using irrigation	9 (5.35)	28 (40.57)
Mean landholding/household (acres)	6.28 (9.06)*	2.48 (2.69)*

*Figures in parentheses are percentages (*Standard Error values). MTR=Melghat Tiger Reserve; BWLS=Bori Wildlife Sanctuary.*

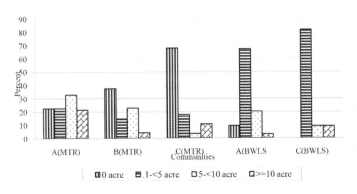

A=Scheduled tribes; B=Scheduled and backward classes; C=Agropastoralists.

Fig. 2: Landholding pattern across communities in Melghat Tiger Reserve (MTR) and Bori Wildlife Sanctuary (BWLS)

As far as the landholding was concerned the mean landholding size was higher for MTR (6.28 acres) compared to BWLS (2.48 acres). Some of the landless households in MTR and BWLS rented land to grow cash crops (Table 3). Majority of the landholders were marginal or small (Fig. 2). Moreover, there was significant difference in the mean landholding size across communities in the two PAs (Kruskal-Wallis 1-way ANOVA: $\chi^2 = 65.8036$, p< 0.01).

Livestock ownership pattern

There was significant difference ($\chi^2 = 38.4193$, p< 0.01) between average livestock per family which varied between 7.24 in MTR to 10.76 in BWLS, with more than 80 per cent of the families owning livestock in both the PAs. The livestock holding however was up to nine cattle per family for the agriculturists. For the agro-pastoralists however, was much larger that is up to 23 cattle per family (Fig. 3).

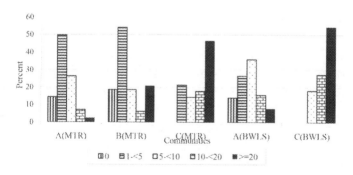

A=Scheduled tribes; B=Scheduled and backward classes; C=Agro-pastoralists.

Fig. 3: Livestock holding pattern across communities in Melghat Tiger Reserve (MTR) and Bori Wildlife Sanctuary (BWLS)

The population structure of livestock showed the number of bulls to be similar across all communities. The number of calves, per family ranged from 0.35 to 6.5 across the communities (χ^2 = 92.9484, p< 0.01) with all the three communities in MTR having a value of $\leq$0.71 calves per family. Families in BWLS had more than 2 calves per family. The number of milk cattle per family were significantly different (χ^2 = 74.2336, p$\leq$ 0.01), especially for the agro-pastoralists in both MTR and BWLS with 14 or more milk cattle per family, compared to agriculturists who had less than 3 milk cattle per family.

Economy and occupation

The local economy was basically a subsistence economy with agriculture primarily for domestic consumption and only the surplus was sold or exchanged in weekly markets for commodities like salt, pepper, oil, etc. The local communities also depended on forest produce for their sustenance, especially during monsoons. By the end of summer the previous year's agricultural produce was exhausted and the new crop was not yet harvested. Moreover the roads were cut off in remote villages, making it necessary for the people to depend on the forest.

The extent of people's dependence on the forests can be seen from the seasonal calendar which brings out the importance of forests in the forest-based economy of the local communities (Table 4). Most of the local communities both tribal and non-tribal in the two PAs, except the agro-pastoralists of MTR, followed the same activity pattern. Moreover, it can also be seen that the local communities were engaged in some or the other forest related activity throughout the year. In areas where the forest had become degraded, agriculture and labour activities also formed a source of income.

Dependence on forest resources

All the communities residing within Melghat Tiger Reserve and Bori Wildlife Sanctuary were dependent on the forest resources both directly and indirectly. For the purpose of this study dependence was considered as "lack of alternatives", either due to non-availability or due to lack of purchasing power. While direct economic dependence was in the form of their requirement for domestic consumption, indirect dependence was more of derived requirement. Direct economic dependence on the forest was for 1) fuel wood; 2) timber, bamboo, leaves and grasses, etc. for house construction, fencing, agricultural implements and thatching; 3) fruits, seeds, forest vegetables, mushrooms, roots, tubers, bamboo shoots, fishes, crabs, etc., for sustenance; and 4) water and pasturing of cattle.

Indirect dependence on the forest was for 1) cultivation and income from the sale of agricultural surplus; 2) income from sale of commercial NTFP and head-loading fuel wood; 3) income from the sale of dairy products; and 4) income from forest related and alternate employment opportunities, within the PAs.

Azra Musavi

Table 4: Seasonal calendar of subsistence activities of sampled households in Melghat Tiger Reserve and Bori Wildlife Sanctuary

Activity Pattern	Months											
	J_1	F	M	A	M	J_2	J_3	A*	S	O	N	D
Cultivation & Agriculture	*	*	*				*	*	*	*	*	*
Collection of Mahua flowers & seeds			*	*		*	*					
Collection of Tendu leaves				*	*							
Collection of tubers, bamboo shoots, mushrooms, etc.						*	*	*	*			
Collection of grasses & fodder	*									*	*	*
Agricultural labour	*	*	*				*	*	*			
Forest labour		*	*		*	*					*	*
Repair of houses, fence, agricultural implements, etc.					*	*						
Storage of fuel wood	*	*	*	*	*	*					*	*
Fishing	*	*	*					*	*	*	*	*

(J1=January; F=February; M=March; A=April; M=May; J2=June; J3=July; A*=August; S=September; O=October; N=November; D=December).

While fuel wood and timber was used by all, irrespective of community or economic status, NTFP was extracted in different intensities by different communities across the two PAs. Similar was the case for dependence on forest for grazing the cattle and collection of leaf fodder, however, the pattern varied between the agro-pastoralists and the agriculturists.

Fuel wood use and seasonality

Wood was used both for cooking purposes, heating water and for keeping the houses warm during monsoons and winters (Average winter temperature = 12° C). No alternative sources of energy were used by any of the sampled households. Although livestock dung was used for lighting fire during the monsoons when the wood was moist, it was not used as fuel. Agricultural residue was left in the field for the livestock and whatever remained after that was burnt in the field as it helped to provide ash. As far as fuel wood consumption was concerned, there was difference in per capita consumption across different communities (daily: $\chi^2 = 63.3167$, p< 0.01; annual: $\chi^2 = 63.0798$, p< 0.01), being highest for agriculturists with assorted professions. On the whole, all the communities in MTR had higher per capita fire wood consumption as compared to the communities in BWLS (Table 5).

Wood was also used for heating the houses during monsoon and winter months. Most of the families were found to be using large logs of wood to light fire at night and to keep themselves warm. Annually each family was found to be using more than 30 quintals (34.35 quintals ±4.53) for heating the houses. Except for a very few who were in government jobs or had an assured source of income used blankets and woollen clothes to keep warm.

Table 5: Fuel wood consumption pattern in sampled households across communities in Melghat Tiger Reserve and Bori Wildlife Sanctuary

Communities		Daily consumption (kg)	Annual consumption (kg)
MTR	A	2.30 (±0.09)	839.19 (±33.60)
"	B	2.76 (±0.19)	1007.86 (±68.58)
"	C	2.13 (±0.28)	776.41 (±100.93)
BWLS	A	1.28 (±0.12)	468.57 (±42.12)
"	C	1.22 (±0.21)	445.19 (±76.32)

All values are mean per capita consumption. Figures in parentheses are Standard Error values.

MTR=Melghat Tiger Reserve; BWLS=Bori Wildlife Sanctuary; A=Scheduled Tribes; B=Scheduled Castes and Backward Classes; C=Agro-pastoralists.

Extraction of non-timber forest products

Non- timber forest produce formed a very important aspect of the rural economy in Melghat and Bori. All communities except the agro-pastoralists in Melghat collected most of the non-timber forest produce with *Madhuca latifolia* flower being the major NTFP being collected. While *Terminalia chebula* (hirda) seed and *Chlorophytum tuberosum* (safed musli) were collected (for sale only) in Melghat, fruits of *Emblica officinalis* (aonla), *Mangifera indica* (aam), *Syzygium cummini* (jamun) and *Diospyros melanoxylon* (tendu) were collected by households in Bori sanctuary only (Table 6). Total quantity of NTFP collected per family had significant differences between communities across the two protected areas ($\chi^2 = 65.1983$, $p< 0.01$) (Table 7). Two of the commercial NTFPs i.e., *Terminalia chebula* (Hirda) and *Chlorophytum tuberossum* (Safed musli) however, did not show significant difference.

It was observed that different NTFPs had different importance in terms of their commercial values (Table 8). Certain NTFPs were collected for domestic consumption and were therefore categorised as non-commercial items, e.g., bamboo shoots, mushrooms, tubers, forest vegetables, fruits of *tendu*, mango and *jamun*, fish and crabs. Some were at times exchanged for other commodities (especially grains, etc.). Some households also caught fish and sold it in the local weekly market (Table 8).

Table 6: Annual collection of non-timber forest products by sampled households in Melghat Tiger Reserve and Bori Wildlife Sanctuary

Major items	MTR			BWLS	
	A	B	C	A	C
Madhuca latifolia flower	92.97	78.63	-	113.73	125.91
	(±8.7)	(±11.6)		(±10.8)	(±26.7)
Madhuca latifolia seed	8.43	5.92	-	17.42	1.45
	(±1.8)	(±2.5)		(±8.2)	(±1.5)
Buchanania lanzan seed	0.54	-	-	3.95	0.09
	(±90.3)			(±1.6)	(±0.1)
Terminalia chebula seed	0.77	2.08	-	-	-
	(±0.6)	(±2.08)			
Emblica officinalis fruit	-	-	-	10.84	-
				(±4.1)	
Diospyros melanoxylon leaves*	13.57	20.83	-	554.45	1225
	(±10.6)	(±15.4)		(±78.7)	(±370.0)
Chlorophytum tuberosum roots	0.05	-	-	-	-
	(±0.03)				

*The values are mean quantity collected/household in kilograms. The figures in parentheses are Standard Error values. MTR=Melghat Tiger Reserve; BWLS=Bori Wildlife Sanctuary; A=Scheduled Tribes; B=Scheduled Castes and Backward Classes; C=Agro-pastoralists. Local names of the various items are given in Appendix-VI. *Diospyros melanoxylon leaves were collected and quantified in bundles; each bundle had 100 leaves and 100 bundles fetch a sum of Rs.30.*

Table 7: Chi-square values for quantities of non-timber forest products collected by sampled households in Melghat Tiger Reserve and Bori Wildlife Sanctuary

Major items	χ^2 values	p values
Madhuca latifolia flowers	56.0902	<0.01
Madhuca latifolia seeds	21.2459	<0.01
Buchanania lanzan seeds	30.1019	<0.01
Terminalia chebula seeds	2.4455	0.6544
Emblica officinalis fruit	45.0603	<0.01
Diospyros melanoxylon leaves	232.5785	<0.01
Chlorophytum tuberosum	2.7297	0.6040

Kruskal-Wallis one-way ANOVA was used to test for differences between the communities in Melghat Tiger Reserve and Bori Wildlife Sanctuary.

Local names of the various items are given in Appendix-VI.

Table 8: Annual sale of non-timber forest products by sampled households in Melghat Tiger Reserve and Bori Wildlife Sanctuary

Communities		Quantity sold (Kg)	Income earned (Rs)
		Madhuca indica flowers	
MTR	A	28.52 (±5.20)	157.38 (±34.89)
"	B	30.96 (±9.70)	91.71 (±29.51)
BWLS	A	12.66 (±3.82)	45.94 (±14.59)
"	C	92.73 (±25.98)	327.36 (±95.16)
		Madhuca indica seeds	
MTR	A	0.13 (±0.08)	0.80 (±0.49)
BWLS	A	10.86 (±7.90)	73.28 (±55.18)
		Buchanania lanzan fruits	
MTR	A	0.34 (±0.22)	4.90 (±3.72)
BWLS	A	3.67 (±1.63)	106.92 (±58.22)
		Terminalia chebula seeds	
MTR	A	0.77 (±0.61)	0.66 (±0.37)
"	B	2.08 (±2.08)	7.29 (±7.29)
		Emblica officinalis fruits	
BWLS	A	10.84 (±4.08)	57.31 (±24.47)
		Diospyros melanaxylon leaves*	
MTR	A	13.57 (±10.59)	4.07 (±3.18)
"	B	20.83 (±15.40)	6.25 (±4.62)
BWLS	A	554.45 (±78.65)	187.39 (±31.52)
"	C	1225 (±370.02)	357.27 (±111.70)
		Chlorophytum tuberosum roots	
MTR	A	0.05 (±0.03)	4.94 (±3.33)

* Diospyros melanoxylon leaves are in bundles. All values are mean annual income from sale of NTFP items/household. The figures in parentheses are the Standard Error values. Local names of the various items are given in Appendix-VI. MTR=Melghat Tiger Reserve; BWLS=Bori Wildlife Sanctuary; A=Scheduled Tribes; B=Scheduled Castes and Backward Classes; C=Agropastoralists.

Grazing pattern

Livestock grazing pattern also reflected differences in basic lifestyles of the different communities in MTR and BWLS. While all the livestock grazed in the forest, those belonging to the agriculturist communities in both PAs, stayed in the forest only during the day hours and it grazed as part of a common village herd. The livestock of agro-pastoralist community in BWLS spent slightly longer time in the forest as they were sent out before day-break and would return by late evening, mostly unaccompanied during early hours. However, the livestock belonging to the agro-pastoralists in MTR spent maximum time in forest as it often camped in the forest, especially at the end of monsoon and during early winter, in temporary cattle camps called "*haites*" occupied and operated by family members, mostly adult males and young boys.

It was also observed that the young calves were stall fed with green leaf fodder. Also, the bulls especially the ones used for ploughing the fields were mostly stall-fed with green fodder and agricultural produce and were rarely sent for grazing with the herds. Although grasses were cut and stored for summers, *Terminalia tomentosa* and *Ficus glomerata* were used as green fodder throughout the year, which was supplemented by any available agricultural by-products. Moreover, after the crops were harvested, the livestock was allowed to graze on the agricultural residue left in the fields. This supplemented the diet of the livestock. Moreover, cattle dung was used as manure in agricultural field.

Table 9: Stall-feed requirements for milk cattle in sampled households of Melghat Tiger Reserve and Bori Wildlife Sanctuary

Communities		Number of milch cattle/ family	Total feed requirement/ day (kg)	Roughage requirement/ day (kg)	
				Dry	Green
MTR	A	2.3 (±0.38)	57.5	32.34	10.78
	B	1.7 (±0.57)	42.5	23.90	7.96
	C	18.1 (±3.36)	452.5	254.53	84.84
BWLS	A	2.5 (±0.44)	62.5	35.15	11.71
	C	14.0 (±3.75)	350	196.87	65.62

The figures in parentheses are Standard Error values. Daily feed and roughage requirements have been worked out per family. MTR=Melghat Tiger Reserve; BWLS=Bori Wildlife Sanctuary; A=Scheduled Tribes; B=Scheduled Castes and backward Classes; C=Agro-pastoralists.

Although no feeding trials were carried out, estimates for stall-feeding of milk cattle only were worked out for the study, as they formed the largest proportion of the total livestock both in MTR and BWLS. Since the approximate weight of free ranging cattle is about 250 kg (stall-fed milk cattle would at least weigh 300 kg), 10% of which should be given as feed (Ranjan, 1986) i.e., 25 kg of feed for the animal to be able to produce 10 litres per day. Out of the total feed requirement, 3 parts should be of roughage while 1 part should be concentrate. The roughage comprises both 'dry' and 'green' fodder. Most of the roughage requirement can be obtained from the agricultural residue and fodder from the forest, in terms of grasses and leaves. Most of the 'concentrates' however have to be purchased. On the basis of the standard feed requirements the quantities for stall-feed milk cattle were worked out for the two study areas (Table 9). While the demand per family for daily feed requirement of the milk cattle varied from 42.5 kg (for Community B in MTR) to 452.5 kg (for Community C in

MTR), 75% of this is comprised of roughage, which can be obtained from agricultural residue and the forest. Thus annually the demand per family for forest based fodder varied from 2.9 tonnes [(7.96 kg × 365 days) ÷ 1000] for Community B in MTR to 30.96 tonnes [(84.84 kg × 365 days) ÷ 1000] for Community C in MTR.

Sources of Income

The local communities were dependent on four major sources of income, which were mostly forest-based however, contribution of income by different sources differed across the communities (Tables 10 and 11). While labour employment was a major source of income for all agricultural communities, dairy activities contributed the most for the agro-pastoralists. In percentage terms while contribution of dairy was 4% to 24% for agriculturists, it was 46% to 84% for agro-pastoralists.

Labour was a major source of income for most households in both PAs. It contributed more than 50% of income of the agriculturist households in both MTR and BWLS and 33% for agro-pastoralists in BWLS. For agro-pastoralists in MTR the contribution of labour to the annual income of a household was only 4% as they were predominantly engaged in cattle rearing and related activities (Fig. 4). Agriculture contributed 9% to 10% for agriculturists and 3% for agro-pastoralists in MTR as most of the families practiced subsistence agriculture. Income from this sector was entirely missing for both communities in Bori as they rarely sold the agricultural produce and were forthcoming in their responses in this regard. Contribution of other sources, i.e., jobs and business ranged from 15% to 17% for A and C in Bori and Community B in MTR.

Table 10: Annual household income of sampled households from different sources in Melghat Tiger Reserve and Bori Wildlife Sanctuary

MTR			BWLS	
A	**B**	**C**	**A**	**C**
Non-timber forest produce				
174	105	-	455	712
(±35.26)	(±29.84)		(±124.33)	(±189.72)
Dairy				
1979	963	19008	1365	5067
(±515.35)	(±432.14)	(±4974.61)	(±376.92)	(±1514.21)
Labour				
17368	15570	819	3013	3690
(±1003.95)	±1188.08)	(±1580.23)	(±169.15)	(±583.27)
Agriculture				
2484	1959	662	-	-
(±346.53)	(±486.27)	(±236.88)		
Others				
717	3888	2177	859	1636
(±258.20)	(±1285.82)	(±932.42)	(±385.51)	(±1636.36)
Total income				
20383	21075	22666	5726	11106
(±988.19)	(±1993.90)	(±4512.35)	(±705.32)	(±2286.76)

All values are in Rupees. The figures are mean income/household. Figures in parentheses are Standard Error values. MTR=Melghat Tiger Reserve; BWLS=Bori Wildlife Sanctuary; A=Scheduled Tribes; B=Scheduled Castes and Backward Classes; C=Agro-pastoralists.

Table 11: Chi-sq. values for contribution of different sources of income for sampled households in Melghat Tiger Reserve and Bori Wildlife Sanctuary

Source of income	χ^2 values	P values
Non-timber forest produce	102.2910	<0.01
Dairy	81.4753	<0.01
Labour	209.8363	<0.01
Agriculture	75.7110	<0.01
Others	23.6062	<0.01
Total income	110.1452	<0.01

Kruskal-Wallis one-way ANOVA was used to test for differences between the communities in Melghat Tiger Reserve and Bori Wildlife Sanctuary.

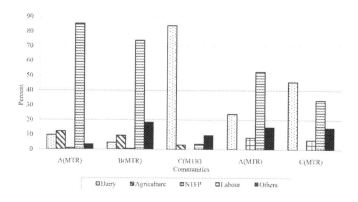

A=Scheduled tribes; B=Scheduled and backward classes; C=Agro-pastoralists; NTFP=Non-timber forest produce.

Fig. 4: Income pattern across communities in Melghat Tiger Reserve (MTR) and Bori Wildlife Sanctuary (BWLS)

Discussion

The findings of the study not only brought out differences in the functioning of government agencies across the two PAs i.e., MTR and BWLS, but also showed the differences in the lifestyles of the various community groups especially the agro-pastoralists and agriculturists (scheduled tribes, scheduled castes and backward classes). Moreover, the level of dependence on forest and its resources was found to be both, the outcome of lifestyles as well as the accessibility / remoteness of the PA from the urban centres.

There were some differences in the working atmosphere which influenced the capabilities of government agencies in MTR and BWLS. However, MTR was better off as it the villages were under the administration of the revenue department and hence more funds were available for their development. Further 5% of the forest revenue was earmarked and available to the *zilla parishad* for supporting development programmes of the villages. In BWLS, civic bodies were missing as the villages in the sanctuary were forest villages. The forest department though traditionally had adequate planning for managing village amenities, it did not have the requisite funds for such programmes for these villages, or for employing the local people satisfactorily in income generating activities. At times funds were even not available for making payments to the local people for work done by them, as the flow of funds to the forest department was significantly inadequate.

Despite the facilities provided for school education in both the PAs, most of the children from tribal households were not interested in attending regular school. The various factors contributing to this pattern were- lack of motivation, as they did not see any permanent / regular employment opportunities in the future; the atmosphere in the tribal household which was not geared towards educating children; and the need for children to help their parents in earning money for the family through labour activities. Lack of accountability for school teachers was perhaps responsible for their disinterest and irregularity in teaching, especially in the remote villages, this resulted in lack of motivation in both the children and their parents. The situation in *ashram* schools (boarding schools run by private organisations in MTR) was different as they were more conscientious about their duties and there was a higher class attendance. These schools were however present only in Melghat.

The demographic characteristics between the two PAs differed slightly in terms of higher number of adults per family in MTR as compared to higher number of children in BWLS. This difference was perhaps a reflection of the success of Family Planning Programme in MTR, rather than a conscious decision on the part of the local people. The author had the opportunity to interact with several men and women on the issue of family size in MTR, especially the relatively large landholders, who showed a comparatively higher family size. They did not seem concerned that their landholding would get fragmented, making them less viable for each of the successive generations. On the contrary, they felt they had enough land and did not seem worried about the future. However, the younger generation showed slightly greater awareness of the need for a smaller family size.

The lower mean family size in BWLS could perhaps be explained by higher overall mortality in the sanctuary villages due to lack of medical facilities. The situation worsened during monsoons, when the entire sanctuary and adjoining areas were inundated due to the overflowing of the numerous streams and rivers which crisscrossed the area. This was also the time when people depended on the forest for most of their food requirements, as the agricultural produce, of the previous year was exhausted and the landless were virtually without any income. Also their houses were most of the time damp. All these factors were responsible for the spread of illness and disease among the local inhabitants. Further, the absence of timely medical aid added to the woes of these people.

The large landholders, especially from the tribal communities in MTR, lived in joint families. This was reflected in the larger family size of this community in which more than two generations resided within the same household and shared a common kitchen. Moreover, the tribal communities in both PAs had higher number of children per family. This was either due to their lack or inadequate awareness to family planning programmes, as compared to other communities.

The family profile and distribution of responsibilities within a family showed that the society was male dominated. This view was further supported by the fact that it was usually men who were the decision makers. Moreover, in any interaction with both men and women, the latter usually had to be coaxed to speak up. Apart from this, women were heavily burdened with household duties. They had to meet their families' needs of fuel, water, food, fodder and thatching, in addition to sharing the workload with the male members during agricultural season. They also worked as wage labourers to earn a living for their families. The decreasing forests and non-availability of potable water in the village vicinity made their tasks more difficult as they had to walk longer distances to fetch fuel wood and water. Mahendra *et al.*, (1992) in their study also came up with similar findings. Women according to this study spent about 3 to 6 hours per day for fuel wood collection.

During the British period, the forest-land was given to the local people to encourage settlements within the forest. This helped in easy supply of labour for logging operations. Consequently, majority of the households belonging to the agriculturist communities, especially in MTR, owned land. With the establishment of the PAs in these regions, landholders who did not have proper "*pattas*" or land deeds lost their landholding, since these were considered as encroachments by the Forest Department. In BWLS, however, quite a few of the families lost their landholding when their agricultural fields came under the back waters of the *Tawa* reservoir. Although they were promised alternative land in other villages within the sanctuary, it was not given to them. This led to landlessness of these families. In addition to these factors, the inherent procedures resulted in some inefficiency in land transfer, thus causing hardships for the successors who were not able to secure control of their land. This essentially led to inter family disputes.

The agro-pastoral communities in MTR had fewer landholders as they were recent entrants in these villages and therefore could not legally acquire land. In BWLS, however, the agro-pastoralists were able to acquire land due to several factors *viz.*, they had been living in the area for almost two to three generations and remoteness of the sanctuary.

The scheduled tribes and scheduled castes (agriculturist communities) families, who owned neither land nor livestock, were completely dependent on labour and other employment opportunities. At times, they rented land to grow cash crops. However, none of the agro-pastoralist families were without livestock. This was a reflection of their basic lifestyle and higher level of dependence on dairying and related activities. Thus their primary profession was pastoralism, agriculture being secondary.

As far as landholding pattern was concerned, most of the landholders were in 'marginal' and 'small' categories, i.e., less than 5 acres of land. The landholdings were mostly either along streams or on hill slopes. Both the size and the location of the landholding necessitated traditional agriculture practices. Moreover, lack of finances and other support facilities in this sector were also responsible for the existing agricultural pattern. There was a high dependence on the monsoons and soil moisture due to lack of irrigation facilities.

The livestock holding pattern reflected the importance of livestock for the agro-pastoral community. This was further emphasised by significantly higher number of milk cattle per family for the agro-pastoralists. Thus, for the agro-pastoral community, livestock had been a means of livelihood. However, for the agriculturists, livestock had traditionally been considered as stored wealth to be used in times of need, for providing milk for domestic consumption and for ploughing their fields.

As seen from the results, the resident communities were dependent on the forest of the two PAs. This is a scenario that is prevalent all over the country, with a large percentage of its people dependent on subsistence agriculture on marginal lands within or close to PAs. Local forest-based communities were heavily dependent on forest areas for fuel wood and grazing of livestock, collection of NTFPs, wood and other material for construction of their houses (Saharia, 1984). Fuel wood formed the major item of "dependence on the forest" in MTR and BWLS. In other parts of the country too fuel wood constitutes the largest single source of supply of domestic fuel (Saharia, 1984). Moreover, for the unemployed landless, its collection and sale formed a major source of livelihood. The pattern of fuel wood consumption varied across the communities. It was seen that no alternative fuel was used by either of the communities, even if they had the resources to afford alternative energy sources. Consequently, those with higher standard of living were observed to be spending more on food and consequently consuming more firewood. Comparatively, the landless, especially in the tribal communities used less amounts of fuel wood, as they could afford fewer and very modest meals. Moreover, they migrated to urban areas for long periods in search of employment opportunities from early winter to beginning of monsoons.

In contrast to the fuel wood consumption pattern, wood for heating purposes was used by all families except those with a higher standard of living; they could afford blankets and woollen clothes to keep themselves warm during winter. Moreover, their houses were better built to keep the monsoon rains out thus excluding the need for large logs of wood for heating purposes.

NTFP collection by different communities brought out the importance of this resource in their lives. The agricultural communities greatly depended on NTFPs to support them during the lean periods. NTFPs provided sustenance both to the landholders as well as to the landless during the monsoons; at this time of the year the agricultural reserves of the previous year were over and the new crop had not yet ripened. Moreover, due to the overflowing of the innumerable rivers and streams the villages were completely isolated. Thus the various NTFP items like the new bamboo shoots, mushrooms, the forest vegetables and roots and tubers that came up with the onset of the monsoon, were their only source of sustenance in such times. For the agro-pastoral communities this was not so, as they were dependent on the earnings from the sale of milk. During monsoons, there were plenty of grasses for the livestock to feed on. This resulted in enhanced milk yield and higher income during this season. NTFPs like *Madhuca* and *Buchnania*, which were collected during late winter and early summer, were also missed by the agro-pastoral communities in MTR as they migrated to plains for grazing their livestock from mid-winter to late summer due to scarcity of grasses in the PA.

As far as the fodder requirement for milk cattle holdings across communities was concerned, the agro-pastoralists showed a markedly high level of dependence on forest fodder (up to 10 times more) as compared to other community groups both in MTR and BWLS. This was because of their large livestock holdings of which 60% to 95% were milk cattle. Moreover, the livestock-grazing pattern was also found different across the communities. Livestock belonging to agro-pastoralists, especially in MTR, often camped in the forest from the end of the monsoon to early winter. These campsites were mostly close to some water source. This provided maximum grazing opportunity to their large herds of livestock, as the forest close to most of the villages was highly degraded compared to the forest, which was away from the villages. Consequently, lower energy and time was expended in travelling to and back from these areas. The fodder requirement of agro-pastoralists for their milk cattle holdings showed a markedly high level of dependence (up to 10 times more) on forest fodder as compared to other community groups both in MTR and BWLS. This was mainly because of their large livestock holdings of which 60% to 95% were milk cattle. Thus the pressure exerted on the forest by the agro-pastoralist livestock was much higher. As mentioned above, most of the agro-pastoralists from MTR migrated to plains for about six months till the onset of the monsoons. However, the rest of the livestock stayed within the PAs throughout the year.

Income by different sources showed significant variation across the communities. Agriculture was mostly for subsistence with the major portion of agricultural produce for domestic consumption. Most of the large landholders in MTR were able to sell commercial crops like soya bean, pulses and oil seeds in the market. This greatly enhanced their incomes. On the other hand, small and marginal farmers traded small portions of their agricultural output, in times of need, for essential commodities like salt, chillies, other cereals etc. Thus the percentage contribution of agriculture, in monetary terms, to the overall household income was low or negligible.

Most NTFPs, except *Diospyros* (Tendu) leaves, were collected for domestic consumption. The latter were officially collected in BWLS, under the supervision of the Madhya Pradesh Forest Department. In MTR, however, the collection of these leaves was restricted to reserved forests outside the PA but on several occasions people were found illegally collecting these leaves in peripheral villages. In times of need, small quantities of NTFPs, especially *Madhuca* (Mahua) flowers, were traded for cereals and other essential commodities. Consequently, the overall contribution of NTFPs to total income of a household was low for all communities except agro-pastoralists in MTR; for the latter this source was entirely missing. These agro-pastoralists could not collect or earn an income from the sale of NTFPs as they were not present during most of the collection season. Moreover, the families that stayed back were busy taking care of their large livestock holdings with hardly any time to spare for this activity. The agro-pastoralists in BWLS however, were involved in this activity like the rest of the communities.

Labour activities contributed substantially to the annual household income. For the agro-pastoralists in MTR however, the contribution of this source was very low. This was because they were involved in cattle rearing and very few of them took up labour activities. The agro-pastoralists in BWLS however, did take up labour activities. This was because their earnings from dairying were not substantial due to the remoteness of the area. Consequently they had to depend on alternative sources for supporting their families.

Thus, while all communities were found to be dependent on the forest resources, the pattern of dependence varied across the communities. While for the tribal households, collection and sale of NTFP has been a source of sustenance and income; livestock for them has traditionally been a form of stored wealth. The tribal households in both PAs were found to be very similar in their lifestyles, as they mostly exploited the forests for domestic use, i.e., fuel wood, small timber for house construction and NTFPs like flowers, fruits, seeds, vegetables, roots, tubers, etc. Therefore, their dependence was more due to lack of alternatives rather than for commercial gain.

Agriculturists with assorted professions continued to practice their traditional profession. However, they were progressive enough to diversify into other activities *viz.,* small business in the villages or jobs in public and private sectors. All this can be attributed to higher literacy rate in this community group. They were also dependent on the forest for fuel wood, timber and NTFPs. However, they could probably afford alternatives.

Most of agro-pastoralists, especially the *Gawlis* in MTR did not own land. However, the *Gawlis* in BWLS had substantial landholding. Both the *Gawli* and the *Gaolan* grazed their cattle in the PA forests. Dairy and related activities formed major source of livelihood for them. Therefore, they had large livestock holdings. Agriculture was their secondary profession. They too were dependent on the forest for fuel wood and timber. In addition to this, they also depended on the forest for grazing their livestock. This latter form of dependence was purely for commercial purpose.

Developing countries like India though rich in biological diversity are having severe problems in protecting these resources in the face of rapidly growing human and livestock populations which to a large extent depend on these forests for sustenance due to increasing poverty and lack of alternatives. The situation is worsened as these countries are also subjected to the pressures of 'development' and the 'market forces', leading to increased pressures on the protected areas. Measures to conserve biodiversity must therefore provide economic incentives to the local indigenous communities for the sustainable use of these resources as reported by Dixon and Sherman (1990) and McNeely (1988). This however, is a challenging task in the remote areas of developing countries, where poverty tends to be pervasive and where any economic development depends directly on access to and use of natural resources (Wells, 1995). Thus, while the gravity and the magnitude of the problems are formidable, tackling them on a long term basis through well formulated, adequately funded and properly executed programmes is a possibility (Panwar, 1990). The pattern of resource dependence of both tribal and non-tribal households in MTR and BWLS can also be reversed and reduced by providing viable and appropriate alternatives through implementation of well formulated programmes and schemes.

Chapter 5

Anthropogenic Impact on Forest

India's tropical forests account for more than 80% of the forest cover (Singh and Singh, 1988). More than 50% of these forests are the moist and dry deciduous type. The moist deciduous forests have been preferred for human settlements as they contain richer biodiversity as well as valuable timber species like teak and have sustained permanent agriculture and forest plantations for a long time. Comparatively, plant growth in the dry deciduous forests is limited by prolonged periods of drought. Moreover, these forests are prone to frequent man-made fires. These fires are usually set off by the agro-pastoralists as they promote a new flush of grass. Also, the NTFP collectors light these fires to clear the forest floor, for easy collection of some categories of NTFP. Both types of fires are set off during the dry periods and therefore, have severe negative impact on the forest by destroying the under-storey of shrub cover besides burning herbs and grasses during the period when there already is a shortage of resources for the wild animals. Depending on adaptations, repeated fires affect regeneration of plants and may bring about a change in communities over time.

The tropical forests have however, been degraded due to immense biotic pressure from rapidly growing human and livestock populations. This has resulted in large-scale conversion of these ecosystems to savannah and open grasslands (Singh and Singh, 1988). The forests of MTR and BWLS which belong to the 'Central Indian dry deciduous' and 'South Indian moist deciduous' (Champion and Seth, 1968) forest types respectively, are no exception. These forests are under increasing anthropogenic pressures from people and livestock residing both inside as well as in the adjacent areas. The cutting / lopping of trees, proliferation of weeds (selective grazing leads to increase in proportion of unpalatable species over palatable species) and reduction in ground cover have an adverse impact on the vegetation and wild animals of these forests. An effort was made to assess the impact of the lifestyles of traditional and agro-pastoral communities on the ecosystem of the two protected areas.

Anthropogenic impact data – collection and analysis

Dependence of local people on the forests for fuel wood, grazing of livestock, fodder, grass collection, small timber etc., has an impact on the forest in terms of tree cutting / felling, lopping, reduced ground cover, soil erosion and compaction, proliferation of weeds, etc. Cutting of fuel wood and grazing by livestock removes biomass from the ecosystem and eventually alters species composition, effects which are not compatible with the objectives of a national park (or even a protected area) to maintain ecosystems in their natural state (CNPPA, 1978). Data were collected and analysed to assess the impact of resource exploitation, on the forests of MTR and BWLS.

Resource-use and its impact on the forest were assessed for which both primary and secondary information was collected. While primary data regarding impact of resource-use were collected through sampling in both MTR and BWLS. Biotic pressures were quantified in the disturbed forests of Melghat (DF1) and Bori (DF2) and the undisturbed forest (UF) of Gugamal National Park and Tourism Zone of MTR. The latter was chosen as undisturbed forest because it was free from grazing, cutting and lopping pressures.

Secondary information was collected from the Research Wing of Project Tiger Melghat. For quantifying resource-use and availability of resources in Bori, 4 radial transects were established in the forest around 3 of the sampled villages. Each of these transects were first marked on the topo-sheets in the 4 compass directions. Data on tree layer was collected in circular plots of 10 m radius at every 500 m on these transects. Seedlings and ground cover were measured in 5 random quadrats of 50 × 50 cm each, within the circular plots. During the sampling process in Bori it was found that radial transects were not suitable in an undulating or rugged terrain. Moreover, it was difficult to isolate the pressure of different villages in a situation where villages were scattered across the protected area and the livestock was free ranging. To overcome these limitations, the method was modified for sampling in MTR. Therefore, sampling was carried out in the forest around the villages covered under the socio-economic survey, as well as in Gugamal National Park and Tourism Zone of MTR. This was done by laying plots in disturbed forest (DF1) along the village trails and on random transects in the UF. Data on tree layer were collected in circular plots (of 10 m radius each) at every 200 m interval on these trails. Number of seedlings and ground cover were measured in 4 random quadrates of 50 × 50 cm within the circular plots. Sample size in both Bori and Melghat were calculated by plotting cumulative frequency of tree species on Y-axis against the area sampled on X-axis, using Species-Area curve (Greig-Smith, 1983; and Keel *et al.*, 1993). Sampling was done in 5.36 ha in the DF and 1.97 ha in the UF.

Data were collected on tree species, girth at breast height (GBH) at 1.37 m from the ground, height class, percentage of cutting / lopping, weed abundance, grazing signs, number of seedlings and percentage of ground cover. All plants in 10 m radius plots with a GBH ≥30 cm were considered as trees. All plants with GBH <30 cm and a height of 2.5 m and above, were considered as recruitment class. Plants whose GBH was less than 30 cm and were less than 2.5 m in height were considered as saplings / seedlings.

Sample selection

The forests around the sample villages, as well as, the forest in National Park and Tourism Zone of MTR were selected for sampling. Sampling was carried out in the vicinity of the villages, so as to assess the availability and use of resources by the people. The forest around the villages was therefore considered as disturbed forest (DF: DF1 was in MTR and DF2 was in BWLS). Gugamal NP and Tourism Zone within the Melghat Tiger Reserve constituted the control as they were free of biotic pressures and they were considered as undisturbed forest (UF) for the purpose of the study.

Data analysis

For the purpose of analysis the data on resource-use and its impact on the available resources were pooled area-wise (DF1 and DF2) for all villages. The data for National Park and Tourism Zone (UF) were pooled together. The data collected on tree species in the circular plots were used to calculate 1) Species richness; 2) Species diversity index; 3) Evenness; and 4) Importance Value Index (IVI). The calculations for the above were done as follows:

1) *Species richness*: This is the total number of species (of trees) found in any area (Magurran, 1988). It provided an extremely useful measure of species richness related to DF1, DF2 and UF. Also the number of common species across the three areas were counted.

2) *Species diversity Index*: Species diversity is seen as an indicator of the well being of ecological systems (Magurran, 1988). It is the number of individuals of each species present. Shannon-Wiener index was used for calculating the diversity of tree species present in both the disturbed (DF1 and DF2) and undisturbed forests (UF).

The equation for the Shannon-Wiener diversity index (H') is as follows:

$H' = -\Sigma pi \ln pi$, where pi may be defined as the proportion of individuals (ni) found in the ith species out of total individuals (N) of all species. The value of the Shannon diversity index (H') is usually found to fall between 1.5 and 3.5 and rarely exceeds 4.5 (Magurran, 1988).

3) *Evenness*: This may be defined as equitable or even distribution of all individuals of the available species present in an area.

$E = H' / \ln S$, where E is the measure of evenness, and S is the total number of species. The value of E lies between 0 and 1.0 with 1.0 representing a situation in which all species are equally abundant (Magurran, 1988).

4) *Importance Value Index*: Importance value index, which is the sum of the relative frequency, relative density and relative dominance of a species, was calculated to characterise the vegetation in different forests and reveal its dominance (Keel *et al.*, 1993). The importance value indices (IVI) of all tree species (GBH $\geq$30 cm) for the disturbed (DF1 and DF2) and undisturbed (UF) forests were calculated.

The relative values were calculated as follows:

Relative frequency (Rfreq.) = (no. of plots in which a species occurs ÷ total no. of occurrences of all species) × 100.

Relative density (Rden) = (no. of individuals of a species ÷ total no. of individuals of all species) × 100.

Relative dominance (Rdom) = (basal area of a species ÷ total basal area of all species) ×100.

Where, Basal area = $\pi \times r^2$. While the value of $\pi = 22 \div 7$ and r is the radius of a tree.

Therefore, Importance value index (IVI) = Rfreq + Rden + Rdom.

The data was also analysed to obtain percentage distribution of stems in different girth classes (GBH) and quantify densities of trees, recruitment class and seedlings / saplings in the three areas.

For assessing the impact on the forest in terms of cutting and lopping pressure, grazing intensity and weed proliferation, visual scores were assigned to each plot using the following scale: no pressure = 0; <25% area affected = 1; 25-50% area affected = 2; ≥50% area affected = 3. The mean scores for each area for each pressure category (i.e., cutting / lopping, grazing intensity / weeds) were calculated to obtain the approximate area affected.

Ground cover scores obtained from the quadrat (50 × 50 cm) sampling were also pooled for each area and the mean scores calculated were: no ground cover = 0; <25% ground cover = 1; 25-50% ground cover = 2; ≥50% ground cover = 3.

Non-parametric tests were used to compare the impact of resource-use between disturbed (DF1 and DF2) and undisturbed (UF) forests.

Limitations

Quantification of impact of resource-use and estimation of growth trends was not possible due to non-availability of data for BWLS. Even though the data were available for MTR, there was a possibility of error in estimating growth trends. As far as the data on the impact of resource-use is concerned, a comparison between Bori and Gugamal NP may not be very appropriate as the forest in BWLS was more moist compared to that of Melghat and Gugamal although the dominant species in both areas were same. But since there were no control plots in the case of Bori WLS, as even Satpura NP, which was supposedly out of bounds for the local people and cattle, was freely used by both.

Vegetation characteristics

The forests of Melghat Tiger Reserve (DF1), Gugamal National Park and Tourism Zone in MTR (UF) and Bori Wildlife Sanctuary (DF2) were dominated by teak (*Tectona grandis*) trees, along with its various tree species associates. While most of the trees were leafless starting from late winter (MTR) to early summer (BWLS), there were riverine areas or riparian forests which were green throughout the year. *Tectona grandis* was found to be the most dominant species in all the three areas (Table 12). The next most important species in both DF1 and DF2 was *Terminalia tomentosa* (19.53 and 30.26 respectively), while *Ougenia oogeinensis* (25.25) was the second most important species in the undisturbed forest (UF).

Tree density and diversity

While the overall densities of trees (GBH $\geq$30 cm) in the different forests did not show significant difference (K-W One-way ANOVA: $\chi^2 = 0.8023$, p= 0.6695), the trees in =>60 cm girth class had higher densities for the undisturbed forest (UF) as compared to both disturbed forests (Table 13). On the other hand, the less than 60 cm girth class had higher densities in both disturbed forests. The values of Shannon Weiner Index (H) showed that tree species diversity was however higher for the undisturbed forest, showing a more even distribution of individuals compared to the disturbed forests (Table 14). The comparison between the disturbed and undisturbed forests showed that 32 of the tree species were common between the different forests.

Table 12: Ten most dominant tree species and their respective Importance values (IVI) in disturbed and undisturbed forests of Melghat Tiger Reserve and Bori Wildlife Sanctuary

DF1	UF	DF2
Tectona grandis (146.41)	Tectona grandis (120.28)	Tectona grandis (83.30)
Terminalia tomentosa (19.53)	Ougeinia oojeinensis (25.25)	Terminalia tomentosa (30.26)
Lagestromea parviflora (14.81)	Lagestromea parviflora (15.72)	Diospyros melanoxylon (21.57)
Ougeinia oojeinensis (12.10)	Zizyphus xylopyra (13.94)	Madhuca indica (16.74)
Anogeissus latifloia (9.59)	Garuga pinnata (13.46)	Zizyphus xylopyra (15.03)
Boswelia serrata (8.91)	Terminalia tomentosa (12.00)	Chloroxylon swietiniodes (13.42)
Butea monosperma (8.25)	Grewia tiliaefolia (10.80)	Lannea coromandelica (12.55)
Emblica officinalis (6.55)	Adina cordifolia (7.34)	Butea monosperma (8.46)
Adina cordifolia (6.32)	Anogeissus latifolia (7.23)	Saccopetalum tomentosum (8.15)
Mitragyna parviflora (5.11)	Kydia calycina (6.18)	Emblica officinalis (8.06)

IVI values and scientific and common names of all tree species are given in Appendices-V and VI respectively. DF1=Disturbed forest of Melghat

Azra Musavi

Tiger Reserve; UF=Undisturbed forest of Gugamal National Park and Tourism Zone in Melghat Tiger Reserve; and DF2=Disturbed forest of Bori Wildlife Sanctuary.

Table 13: Density of trees in different girth classes in disturbed and undisturbed forests of Melghat Tiger Reserve and Bori Wildlife Sanctuary

GBH classes	DF1	UF	DF2
30 to <60 cm	207.33 (14.97)	183.71 (19.48)	225.81 (31.45)
60 to <90 cm	86.94 (6.31)	104.08 (9.26)	95.48 (11.25)
90 to <120 cm	58.22 (3.93)	63.17 (4.50)	50.69 (8.08)
≥120 cm	46.97 (4.04)	48.98 (3.99)	59.14 (9.84)
Total	320.87 (14.85)	334.03 (20.97)	318.89 (34.71)

The values are mean densities /ha. The figures in parentheses are Standard Error values.

GBH= Girth at breast height; DF1=Disturbed forest of Melghat Tiger Reserve; UF=Undisturbed forest of Gugamal National Park and Tourism Zone in Melghat Tiger Reserve; and DF2=Disturbed forest of Bori Wildlife Sanctuary.

Table 14: Tree species diversity and richness in disturbed and undisturbed forests of Melghat Tiger Reserve and Bori Wildlife Sanctuary

Area	No. of species (S)	Shannon-Weiner index (H′)	Evenness (E)
DF1	62	2.037251	0.493
UF	48	2.424555	0.626
DF2	47	0.293858	0.076

The value of diversity index (H′) usually lies between 1.5 and 3.5, with higher values showing greater diversity. The value of evenness (E) lies between 0 and 1, with values being closer to 1 showing a more even distribution of species DF1=Disturbed forest of Melghat Tiger Reserve; UF=Undisturbed forest of Gugamal National Park and Tourism Zone in Melghat Tiger Reserve; and DF2=Disturbed forest of Bori WildlifeSanctuary.

Recruitment, shrub cover and regenertion

The recruitment and shrub (GBH <30 cm) densities were significantly higher ($p<0.01$) for disturbed forests of Melghat (DF1) and Bori (DF2) compared to the undisturbed forest (Table 15). Moreover, there were significant differences in the three categories. Although seedling regeneration in all forests was good, it was also significantly high ($p< 0.01$) for undisturbed forest (14501.99 individuals / ha).

Table 15: Recruitment, shrub cover and seedling densities in disturbed and undisturbed forests of Melghat Tiger Reserve and Bori Wildlife Sanctuary

Category	DF1	UF	DF2	χ^2 values
Recruitment and shrub cover	293.54	159.56	594.23	33.1844
	(22.77)	(14.69)	(95.74)	($p<0.01$)
Seedling	3909.77	14501.99	10947.37	60.8464
	(537.02)	(1498.01)	(1576.33)	($p<0.01$)

Kruskal-Wallis one-way ANOVA has been used to calculate χ^2 values. The values are mean densities / ha. The figures in parentheses are Standard Error values. DF1=Disturbed forest of Melghat Tiger Reserve; UF=Undisturbed forest of Gugamal National Park and Tourism Zone in Melghat Tiger Reserve; and DF2=Disturbed forest of Bori Wildlife Sanctuary.

Impact of resource use

The forests of both MTR and BWLS were under anthropogenic pressures in terms of cutting and lopping of trees for fuel wood, timber and fodder. They were also used by the local people for grazing domestic livestock and collecting NTFPs.

Major tree species used by the people

On the basis of information collected from the local people, six major tree species used by the people for fuel wood, fodder, timber and NTFP were identified *viz.*, *Anogeissus latifolia* (dhaora), *Ougeinia oojeinensis* (tiwas), *Terminalia tomentosa* (saj), *Buchanania lanzna* (chironji), *Madhuca indica* (mahua) and *Diospyros melanoxylon* (tendu). The percentage representation of these species in regeneration, recruitment (<30 cm GBH) and tree classes (≥30 cm GBH) out of the total number of stems found in that class was worked out (Table 16).

Table 16: Major tree species used by the people in disturbed and undisturbed forests of Melghat Tiger Reserve and Bori Wildlife Sanctuary

Species	DF1			UF			DF2		
	Seed	Recrt.	Tree	Seed	Recrt.	Tree	Seed	Recrt.	Tree
A. latifolia	9.8	4.4	2.4	14.3	2.2	1.7	2.1	11.4	1.4
O. oojenensis	15.68	3.0	4.4	29.7	9.4	9.5	2.1	0.9	0.6
T. tomentosa	3.92	2.3	4.5	9.9	1.8	2.5	14.6	4.4	9.2
B. lanzan	-	0.9	0.5	-	-	1.2	-	0.9	1.2
M. indica	-	0.2	0.7	-	0.44	1.2	-	1.0	4.6
D. melanoxylon	5.88	2.9	0.9	2.2	1.1	0.3	6.3	16.0	9.8

All the figures are percentage of the total number of stems found in each class i.e., seedling, recruitment (<30 cm GBH) and *tree (≥30 cm GBH). GBH=Girth at breast height. DF1=Disturbed forest of Melghat Tiger Reserve; UF=Undisturbed forest of Gugamal National Park and Tourism Zone in Melghat Tiger Reserve; DF2=Disturbed forest of Bori Wildlife Sanctuary; Seed=Seedling; Recrt.=Recruitment.*

While *Anogeissus latifolia* (dhaora) and *Ougeinia oojeinensis* (tiwas) were primarily used for fuelwood, *Terminalia tomentosa* (saj) was used both for fuel wood, small timber as well as fodder. The last three species, i.e., *Buchanania lanzan* (chironji), *Madhuca indica* (mahua) and *Diospyros melanoxylon* (tendu) were the most important non-timber forest produce species.

Cutting and lopping pressure

Density of cut and / or lopped trees in different girth classes in the three areas was examined. It was found that the girth class of less than 30 cm was found to be most affected in both the disturbed forests of MTR and BWLS followed by 30 cm to 60 cm girth class. The pressure however was not very high on 60 cm and above girth classes. In the undisturbed forest (UF) however, it was the 30 cm to 60 cm girth class which was most affected (Table 17).

Table 17: Density of cut and lopped trees in disturbed and undisturbed forests of Melghat Tiger Reserve and Bori Wildlife Sanctuary

GBH classes	DF1	UF	DF2
<30 cm	133.81 (±11.90)	32.25	161.29 (±26.16)
30 to <60 cm	68.41 (±4.61)	53.76 (±21.50)	91.61 (±12.17)
60 to <90 cm	50.86 (±4.79)	-	57.60 (±6.03)
90 to <120 cm	32.25	-	46.08 (±6.52)
≥120 cm	32.25	-	50.18 (±7.81)
Total	183.77 (±13.58)	64.52 (±32.26)	251.42 (±32.77)

The values are mean densities / ha. The figures in parentheses are Standard Error values. GBH=Girth at breast height; DF1=Disturbed forest of Melghat Tiger Reserve; UF= Undisturbed forests of Gugamal National Park and Tourism Zone in Melghat Tiger Reserve; and DF2=Disturbed forest of Bori Wildlife Sanctuary.

Impact on ground cover

The impact of anthropogenic activities was seen in the significantly lower ground cover (<25%) in the forest around the villages, both in MTR and BWLS. In the undisturbed forest which was free of all pressures, the ground cover was more than 50% (Table 18). In both MTR and BWLS more than 50% of the area of disturbed forests was affected due to grazing by livestock and weed proliferation. The mean score for 'grazing and weed' was highest for the disturbed forest (DF1) of MTR. Moreover, 25-50% of disturbed forests were affected by cutting and lopping of trees by the local people. The forest of BWLS (DF2) however, had highest cutting and lopping pressure. For the undisturbed forest (UF) the mean scores for both the parameters were less than one. Differences in disturbance scores for both parameters were found to be significant at $p < 0.01$ (Table 18).

Intensity of grazing and weed abundance was not significant between the disturbed forest of MTR and BWLS. Cutting and lopping pressures in DF1 and DF2 were however found to be significantly different ($p < 0.01$). Moreover, both cutting and lopping pressure for UF was also significantly different ($p < 0.01$) from those of the disturbed forests (Mann-Whitney U-test values - Table 19).

Table 18: Disturbance and ground cover scores in disturbed and undisturbed forests of Melghat Tiger Reserve and Bori Wildlife Sanctuary

Parameters	DF1	UF	DF2	χ^2 values
Grazing & Weeds	2.14	0.19	2.03	131.6469
	(±0.06)	(±0.06)	(±0.13)	(p<0.01)
Cutting & Lopping	1.56	0.03	2.32	139.7218
	(±0.07)	(±0.02)	(±0.12)	(p<0.01)
Ground cover	1.64	2.31	1.43	115.93
	(±0.04)	(±0.06)	(±0.05)	(p<0.01)

Kruskal-Wallis one-way ANOVA was used to calculate χ^2 values. All the values are mean scores. The figures in parentheses are Standard

*Error values. While 0 = 0%, 1= <25%, 2 = 25-50% and 3= >50%.
DF1=Disturbed forest of Melghat Tiger Reserve; UF=Undisturbed
forest of Gugamal National Park and Tourism Zone in Melghat Tiger
Reserve; and DF2=Disturbed forest of Bori Wildlife Sanctuary.*

Table 19: Mann-Whitney U-test values for disturbance scores in disturbed and undisturbed forests of Melghat Tiger Reserve and Bori Wildlife Sanctuary

Parameters	DF1 and UF	DF1 and DF2	UF and DF2
Grazing & Weeds	-11.0944	-0.7218	8.4932
	(p<0.01)	(p=0.47)	(p<0.01)
Cutting & Lopping	-10.6952	-4.7457	-9.5088
	(p<0.01)	(p<0.01)	(p<0.01)

*Mann-Whitney U-test was used to test for differences between the areas.
The values are Z-statistics.*

*DF1=Disturbed forest of Melghat Tiger Reserve; UF=Undisturbed
forests of Gugamal National Park and Tourism Zone in Melghat Tiger
Reserve; and DF2=Disturbed forest of Bori Wildlife Sanctuary.*

Discussion

The comparison between the disturbed (DF1 and DF2) forests of MTR and BWLS with the undisturbed (UF) forests of Gugamal National Park and Tourism Zone of MTR showed that as many as 32 tree species were common between them. The undisturbed forest showed the highest tree species diversity ($H' = 2.42$). Individuals of these species were more evenly distributed ($E = 0.62$) in the undisturbed forest than in the disturbed forests. Since both diversity and evenness are indices of the level of disturbance, the higher values for undisturbed forest (UF) reflected the low or negligible disturbance or pressure as compared to disturbed forests of Melghat (DF1) and Bori Wildlife Sanctuary (DF2).

Lower diversity values of MTR and BWLS forests as compared to those of other tropical forests (Knight, 1975 and Saxena and Singh, 1982) however, may be attributed to the fact that most of these areas had been worked for timber, especially teak, since the 19th century. Consequently these forests were dominated by teak. In addition to teak there were other associate species *viz., Terminalia tomentosa, Ougeinia oojeinensis, Lagerstroemia parviflora*, etc., as could be seen from the importance value indices (IVI) of tree species.

Uncontrolled human activities in and around PAs lead to degradation of forest ecosystems; grazing by domestic livestock is one of the major causes of forest degradation in India. Other factors like deliberate forest fires, felling / lopping of trees for fuel wood, fodder and timber as well as NTFP collection by local people also affect the forest structure. Findings of this study also revealed that human activities in MTR and BWLS had resulted in overall low tree densities and diversity in the disturbed forests (DF1 and DF2).

Distribution of trees in different girth classes showed a positive trend, with highest density of trees in GBH class '<30 cm' (recruitment class). The next highest density was in GBH class '30 cm to <60 cm', in disturbed forests of Melghat (DF1) and Bori (DF2). This is because of coppicing of cut trees, especially teak and at times *tendu* (in BWLS). In the undisturbed forest (Gugamal National Park and Tourism Zone of MTR) however, all human activities had been stopped since the 1970's. This forest was managed only for wildlife. Consequently it was an old forest, with negligible disturbance caused by human activity. Therefore, it was '30 cm to <60 cm' GBH class which had the highest density in this forest. Thus, it can be expected that if the human pressure is reduced through protective measures the presently disturbed forest would recover and in due course its structure would become similar to that of the undisturbed forest. When the data from permanently marked plots of 1 hectare each (collected by the MTR Research Wing during 1982 to 1994), were used for comparing trends in densities of trees, it was found that over this period, densities of majority of the tree species used by the local people had declined in disturbed forest of Melghat (DF1), however they showed slight increase in the UF as a result of protection. As similar data for BWLS was not available these trends in the three forests could not be compared.

As far as the regeneration class was concerned, the seedling densities in disturbed forests of Melghat (DF1) were significantly ($p< 0.001$) lower compared to undisturbed forests (UF) and disturbed forests of Bori (DF2). The number of saplings and seedlings per unit area help us assess the regeneration potential in different forest types (Saxena and Singh, 1982). The higher seedling density of the undisturbed forests therefore, can be attributed to the protection against all anthropogenic activities. The forests of BWLS also had higher seedling density compared to MTR forest probably due to lower livestock pressure and also because it was a moist deciduous forest type. MTR had a large population of livestock belonging to the *Gawli* families, leading to high cattle densities. Moreover, the cattle belonging to the *Gawlis* grazed deep in the forest, especially during monsoon and early winter, the time when the seeds germinate and the seedlings and saplings grow. Thus, high livestock density along with the grazing pattern had a negative impact on the regeneration of seedlings in MTR forest. Fox (1983) also reported that livestock grazing combined with fodder collection was a major cause of destroying and degrading forest resources in the Middle Hills of Nepal.

Regeneration and recruitment ratios of most commonly used tree species were observed. The species were *Anogeissus latifolia, Ougeinia oojeinensis, Terminalia tomentosa, Buchanania latifolia, Madhuca indica* and *Diospyros melanoxylon*. While the regeneration rates of *Anogeissus latifolia* and *Ougeinia oojeinensis* were markedly lower in both the disturbed forests, *Terminalia tomentosa* had a low regeneration status in disturbed forests of MTR. The recruitment rates ('less than 30 cm' GBH class) of these species, except *Ougeinia oojeinensis* were higher in the disturbed forests due to coppicing of cut stumps. Two of the NTFP species *viz., Buchanania latifolia* and *Madhuca indica* had no representation in the seedling class. This was probably because both these species were under pressure due to collection of the fruits of these species. Apart from that both species are slow growing and naturally occur in low densities. These factors therefore, resulted in reducing their success of regeneration. Slow growth and low abundance could also be the factors responsible for their apparently poor regeneration in the undisturbed forest. Here it is important to mention that the agro-pastoralists return to MTR at the onset of the monsoon and their cattle together with the local cattle graze in the forest (DF1). This has an adverse impact on the ground cover and results in higher seedling mortality. The frequency of both *Buchanania latifolia* and *Madhuca indica*, in recruitment and tree classes was however found to be comparatively higher in BWLS.

Diospyros melanoxylon was also an important NTFP species, especially in BWLS, where the local people collected its leaves under the supervision of the Forest Department. To enhance the production of tender new leaves the local people usually cut the main stem of this tree. This could be the reason for the high percentage of its stems in the recruitment class in disturbed forest of Bori (DF2). The local people also ate its fruit which however had no commercial value. Therefore only small quantities of its fruit were collected, which did not show an adverse impact on its regeneration. Except for the two NTFP species whose seeds were collected, all the other species were found to be regenerating. Most of these species showed low recruitment success. *Buchanania latifolia* and *Madhuca indica* seemed to be the worst affected with almost no regeneration which may directly affect their long term survival, and cause local extirpation.

The impact of people's dependence on the forests for fuel wood, timber and fodder for livestock was reflected in the density of cut and lopped trees in different girth classes in the disturbed forests of Bori and Melghat. The pressure however, was found to be highest on 'recruitment class' (<30 cm GBH) followed by the 'pole class' (30 cm to <60 cm GBH), as these were used for fuel wood and therefore regularly exploited. This girth class is also exploited for small timber which is used for fencing etc. The '90 cm and above' girth classes also showed cutting pressure in the disturbed forests of MTR and BWLS. This was because during monsoon and winter months, large logs of wood were kept burning overnight in the households. Wood was also stored for the monsoon so people cut down larger girth trees instead of collecting fallen wood. Moreover, this girth class was also affected due to extraction of timber in forestry operations in the recent past.

However, in the undisturbed forest (UF) trees in '30 cm to <60 cm' girth class were found to be most affected. This was due to a labour camp within the NP; the labourers were using timber both for fuel as well as for lighting fire at night to keep the wild animals away. Thus the 'pole class' was more suitable for their requirements. The '60 cm and above' girth classes were found to be unaffected in the absence of any anthropogenic pressure in the undisturbed forest. It was seen that while the trees were under pressure both for cutting and lopping, a larger number of the trees were affected by the cutting.

The overall impact of biotic pressure on the forest was in the form of lower ground cover, higher weed abundance, and low seedling densities in both the disturbed forests i.e., DF1 and DF2. In the long run the degradation of forest and inadequate regeneration would likely impede the survival of good quality forest and adversely affect the faunal diversity and richness unless steps are taken to reduce these pressures.

Chapter 6

Spatial Distribution of Biotic Pressure in Melghat Tiger Reserve

In a traditionally agricultural society like India where 80% of the people are dependent upon agriculture and where the population has more than doubled since independence, the pressures on all natural areas are tremendous (Saharia, 1983, Lal, 1989, Anon. 1999, National Forestry Action Programme). The establishment and management of protected areas is one of the most important ways of ensuring conservation of natural resources. However, in most of the developing countries, majority of the PAs are inhabited by indigenous people (MacKinnon, *et al.* 1986), whose sustainability within the PA along with wildlife values is the major challenge to the management of the area (Kothari, *et al.*, 1981; Sarabhai, *et al.*, 1991).

Pressure has been defined by Berkmuller *et al.* (*1986*) as 'use of protected area resources to the extent of creating an adverse impact on its habitat and wildlife'. The impact on forest could be in terms of tree cutting / felling, lopping, reduced ground cover, increased rate of erosion, weed infestation and competition between wildlife and livestock for fodder and water. Dependence of local people on the forests for timber, grazing of livestock, fuel wood, fodder and grasses and other material for construction, as well as fruits, plants, roots, tubers, etc. for sustenance constitutes the 'biotic pressure' on the forests.

Biotic pressure – data collection and analysis

Distribution of biotic pressure on the forests of MTR was assessed for identifying pressure areas. This was done with the intention of bringing in the active participation of the field staff, as well as, of developing it as a management tool for the PAs / managed forests. This exercise was however carried out only for Melghat. All secondary compartment-based information on MTR was collected from the office of Project Tiger, Melghat. This included the list of compartments in various management and administrative zones / units (National Park, Sanctuary, Multiple use areas or the managed forests, Tourism Zone, Satellite cores and the various Rounds) in MTR, the annual block-based wild animal (gaur, sambar, barking deer and wild boar) census data and waterhole counts. Data were collected for all 715 compartments in MTR, from both wildlife and territorial field staff (guards, foresters, rangers).

Data on intensity of impact was collected for ten biotic parameters - grazing, fuel wood collection, lopping for fodder, illicit felling of trees, grass cutting, encroachment, hunting, fishing, fire and waterhole use by domestic livestock. The respondents were asked to rate each compartment, for each biotic parameter separately, on a scale of 0 to 3, where, 0 = no pressure, 1 = >0 - $<25\%$ of the compartment was affected, $2 = 25\text{-}50\%$ of the compartment is under influence and $3 = >50\%$ of the compartment is under influence.

For the purpose of analysis, a median score for each of the 10 biotic parameters was calculated from the available responses for each compartment in MTR. This was done to avoid the influence of any extreme values. Correlations and linear regressions were carried out using the scores for each biotic parameter affecting each compartment to look for relations, if any, between the various parameters.

To prepare compartment wise pressure scores for each of the ten biotic parameters, weighted average (w) for each compartment in a round was calculated as follows:

$w = p \times a$, where $w =$ weighted average of the compartment, $p =$ median pressure score of a compartment for the concerned biotic parameter, i.e., grazing / lopping / fuel wood collection /waterhole use by livestock, etc., $a =$ area of the compartment. The weighted averages for each compartment were then added for the round to arrive at a weighted average pressure score for the round (W) as follows:

$W = Wn \div An$, where $W =$ Weighted average of the round, $Wn =$ Sum of the weighted averages of each of the compartments in the round ($w_1 + w_2 + w_3 + \ldots + w_n$), $An =$ Sum of the areas of all the compartments within the round ($a_1 + a_2 + a_3 + \ldots + a_n$). The weighted averages of the rounds were re-scaled to the six original pressure categories assigned to the compartments as follows:

$W_c = [(W - W_{min}) / (W_{max} - W_{min})] \times 6$, where $W_c =$ re-scaled pressure score for the round, $W =$ Weighted average of the round for each biotic parameter category, $W_{min} =$

lowest weighted average value across all biotic parameters and across all rounds, i.e., '0' in this case. W_{max} = highest weighted average value across all biotic parameters and across all rounds, i.e., '2.25' in this case. Further median pressure scores of the five major biotic factors were averaged for every compartment in MTR. The average score was re-scaled to the original scale (Musavi *et al.*, 2006)

Limitations

This was a subjective method of assessing the influence of various biotic parameters in a PA and therefore, cannot be relied on without crosschecking the information. As the field staff of MTR was doing this exercise for the first time they may not have made an accurate assessment of each compartment. However, if this technique is used annually by the management it could develop into a useful tool for assessing the changes in the influence of various biotic parameters on the PA, both at macro and micro levels.

Management units

MTR was divided into three major management units, the national park (361.52 sq.km.), wildlife sanctuary (777 sq.km.) and the multiple-use area or the MUA managed forests (526.22 sq.km.). Tourism zone, which lies within the wildlife sanctuary, covered an area of 55.87sq.km. In addition to these units there were two proposed satellite cores, one in the east of the sanctuary (Raipur satellite core, approximately 54 sq.km.) and the other is in the north-west of the multiple-use area (Rangubeli satellite core, approximately 34 sq.km.).

Administrative units

The tiger reserve was divided into 4 major administrative units or ranges, namely Chikhaldhara, Dhakna, Harisal and Semadoh. These ranges were further sub-divided into 15 rounds / blocks. The smallest round (Kund) with an area of 41.94sq.km. (19 compartments) had no villages within it. Apart from Kund, Khongda round (27 sq.km.) too did not have any villages located in it. Kolkaz covered an area of 202.35sq.km (83 compartments) with 3 villages located in it. Hatru round however, had the largest number of compartments (91) and also the highest number of villages. The highest human density (34.76 per sq.km.) and livestock density (29.54 per sq.km.) was in the Tarubanda round. Overall there were two rounds with no villages, seven rounds with less than 5 villages, five rounds with 5-10 villages and only one round with more than 10 villages (Tables 20 - 22).

Table 20: Details of villages located adjacent to and within five kilometres of the national park boundary (Melghat Tiger Reserve)

Village	Location	Human population[1]	Livestock population[2]
Bori*	WLS	97	161
Dhargad*	WLS	379	553
Koha*	WLS	296	549
Vairat*	WLS	116	279
Pastalai*	WLS	157	98
Churni*	WLS	113	272
Memna	WLS	109	122
Kelpani	WLS	509	310
Gularghat	WLS	472	336
Dolar	WLS	157	303
Dhakna	WLS	422	388
Adaho	WLS	341	991
Kund	WLS	183	331
Pili	WLS	388	513
Semadoh	WLS	1087	969
Dabia	MUA	233	314
Saori	MUA	282	726
Garga Bhandum	MUA	265	224

Tarubanda	MUA	352	491
Total (19)		5958	7930

*Villages located adjacent to the National Park boundary. [1] Population census 1991.
[2] Livestock census 1993. WLS = Wildlife Sanctuary, MUA = Multiple-use area.*

Table 21: Summary of villages in Melghat Tiger Reserve

Parameters	Sanctuary	Multiple-use area
Number of villages	22	39
Human population (1991)	7989	15269
Human density (per km^2)	11.07*	29.01
Livestock population (1993)	9687	15057
Livestock density (per km^2)	13.43*	28.67

*Density figures were calculated by excluding the area of tourism zone
(55.87 sq.km. in GIS domain) from the total area of the sanctuary (777
sq.km in GIS domain), i.e., an area of 721.13 sq.km. This was done as no
extractive activities were allowed in the tourism zone.*

Table 22: Details of rounds in Melghat Tiger Reserve

Round/ blocks	Area*	Compartments	Villages
Jarida	133.31	66	10
Hatru	189.87	91	11
Kuwapati	107.07	66	1
Kolkaz	202.35	83	3
Rangubeli	110.31	47	5
Harisal	137.14	56	5
Tarubanda	98.62	46	10
Kund	44.01	19	0
Chikhaldara	69.86	36	4
Khongda	48.51	27	0
Koha	71.19	31	1
Dhakna	114.56	43	6
Dolar	64.69	36	1
Koktu	65.98	41	1
Dhargad	89.96	27	3

*Area is map area in square kilometres. **Per sq.km density was
calculated from the 1991 population census figures. *** Per sq.km
density was calculated from the 1993 livestock census figures.*

Biotic Pressure

As mentioned in earlier sections, villages were located inside MTR except in the National Park and Tourism Zone. Consequently, the human and livestock populations of these villages were totally dependent on the forests of the Protected Area for their sustenance. This exerted a high degree of biotic dependence on MTR. Impact of 10 major biotic parameters was therefore assessed both at the level of management units (Table 23) as well as the administrative units, i.e., the rounds (Table 24).

Grazing by livestock

More than 80% of the compartments in Sanctuary and MUA were under the influence of grazing, while in the NP and tourism zone (TZ) only 5% and 20% respectively were under grazing pressure. As far as the grazing pressure in the rounds was concerned more than 90% i.e. 4 out of 15 rounds were affected by grazing by livestock. Jarida, Hatru and Tarubanda rounds had the highest grazing pressure with more than 75% of the area under grazing. The lowest pressure was in Dolar round where less than 12.5% of the area was being grazed. Khongda however, was the only round which was free of grazing pressure.

Table 23: Distribution of biotic pressure across management zones

Parameters	Sanctuary	Multiple-use Area	National Park	Tourism Zone
Grazing– Affected (%)	266 (86.3)	226(99.5)	7(4.6)	5(20)
Not affected (%)	42(13.6)	1 (0.4)	148(95.4)	20(80)
Lopping– Affected (%)	206(66.8)	167(73.5)	6(3.8)	1(4)
Not affected (%)	102(33.1)	60(26.4)	149(96.1)	24(96)
Fuelwood collection– Affected (%)	173(56.1)	179(78.8)	11(7)	1(4)

Not affected (%)	135(43.8)	48(21.1)	144(92.9)	24(96)
Illicit felling– Affected (%)	171(55.5)	168(74)	2(1.2)	1(4)
Not affected (%)	137(44.4)	59(25.9)	153(98.7)	24(96)
Grass cutting– Affected (%)	132 (42.8)	104(45.8)	14(9)	9(36)
Not affected (%)	176(57.1)	123(54.1)	141(90.9)	16(64)
Waterhole use– Affected (%)	175 (56.8)	96(42.2)	8(5.1)	4(16)
Not affected (%)	133(43.1)	131(57.7)	147(98.4)	21(84)
Fire– Affected (%)	206(66.8)	124(54.6)	20(12.9)	15(60)
Not affected (%)	102(33.1)	103(45.3)	134(86.4)	10(40)
Fishing– Affected (%)	124(40.2)	86(37.8)	6(3.8)	3(12)
Not affected (%)	184(59.7)	141(62.1)	149(96.1)	22(88)
Hunting– Affected (%)	109(35.3)	61(26.8)	1(0.6)	0
Not affected (%)	199(64.6)	166(73.1)	154(99.3)	25(100)
Encroachment– Affected (%)	34(11)	40(17.6)	0	0
Not affected (%)	274(88.9)	187(82.3)	155(100)	0

Lopping

More than 65% of the compartments in Sanctuary and MUA were subjected to lopping, while in NP and TZ less than 5% of the compartments were under lopping pressure. Round-wise lopping pressure showed a similar distribution with 14 out of 15 rounds (>90%) affected by the activity. Lopping pressure was highest for Rangubeli, Tarubanda, Harisal and Kund rounds. While Khongda was free of lopping pressure, seven of the rounds showed low intensity lopping, with no rounds in ≥37.5% affected area categories pressure.

Table 24: Weighted average scores* for grazing, lopping, fuel wood collection, illicit felling, grass cutting, waterhole use by livestock, incidence of fire, fishing, hunting and encroachment across different blocks / rounds in Melghat Tiger Reserve

Rounds	G	L	FW	IF	GC	WH	FR	FH	H	EN
Jarida	6	2	4	2	1	3	3	1	1	1
Hatru	6	1	2	2	1	2	2	1	1	1
Kuwapati	4	2	2	2	1	2	2	2	1	0
Kolkaz	4	2	2	1	2	2	3	1	1	1
Rangubeli	4	3	3	3	1	2	3	2	2	1

Harisal	5	3	3	2	1	1	1	1	1	1
Tarubanda	6	3	4	2	2	3	1	2	1	1
Kund	2	3	1	1	1	2	1	1	1	0
Chikhaldara	2	1	1	1	1	1	1	1	1	1
Khongda	0	0	1	0	1	0	1	1	0	0
Koha	4	1	2	1	3	4	2	1	0	0
Dhakna	5	1	2	1	1	1	1	1	1	1
Dolar	1	1	1	1	1	1	1	1	1	1
Koktoo	2	1	1	1	1	1	1	1	1	1
Dhargad	4	1	2	2	1	2	1	1	1	1

* *0=no presssure, 1=very low (>0 - <12.5%), 2=low (12.5 - <25%), 3=medium (25 - <37.5%), 4=moderately high (37.5 - <50%), 5=high (50 – 75%), 6=very high (>75%).*

G=Grazing; L=Lopping; FW=Fuel wood collection; IF=Illicit felling; GC=Grass cutting; WH=Waterhole use by livestock; FR=Incidence of Fire; FH=Fishing; H=Hunting; EN=Encroachment.

Fuel wood collection

While 56% and 79% of the compartments in sanctuary and MUA respectively were affected due to fuel wood collection, less than 10% of the compartments in NP and TZ were affected. Fuel wood collection pressure was highest for Jarida and Tarubanda rounds, while Kund, Chikhaldara, Khongda, Dolar and Koktoo rounds showed very low intensity of pressure. While fuel wood collection activity was reported for every round, there was no round in the high or very high-pressure category i.e., ≥50% of the round / block area under fuel wood collection.

Illicit felling

While 55% of the compartments in sanctuary and 74% in MUA were affected by illicit felling of trees in the forest, only 1% and 4% in the NP and TZ respectively showed illicit tree felling. While Rangubeli round / block had the highest tree felling pressure, on the whole 13 out of 15 rounds showed very low to low intensity of illicit tree felling.

Grass cutting

Grass cutting showed a slight reversal of the pattern for the preceding biotic parameters, with all the management zones showing less than 40% of compartments in the affected category. Moreover, as far as the NP and TZ were concerned, the percentage of compartments affected by grass cutting was marginally higher compared to those affected by other biotic activities. While 12 out of the 15 blocks / rounds showed very low intensity of grass cutting, the remaining 3 rounds showed low to medium intensity of grass cutting.

Waterhole use by livestock

More than 50% of the compartments showed use of waterholes by domestic livestock in the sanctuary however, in the MUA only 42% of the compartments were affected by this biotic activity. In NP only 5% of the compartments showed waterhole use by domestic livestock, in TZ 16% of the compartments were affected. While Khongda round was free of waterhole usage by domestic livestock, five of the rounds showed very low intensity of waterhole use and Koha round showed moderately high waterhole use. Six of the rounds / blocks showed low intensity waterhole use.

Fire

Incidence of fire was reported from more than 50% of the compartments in sanctuary, MUA and TZ. In the NP area however, fire was reported only from 13% of the compartments. Round-wise Jarida, Kolkaz, and Rangubeli showed medium intensity of fire. Nine out of 15 rounds showed very low intensity fire with Khongda and Dhargad rounds showing negligible fire. The remaining three rounds were affected by low intensity fire.

Fishing and Hunting

Both fishing and hunting for domestic purpose or to sell in local markets was reported from all the management zones. While fishing was reported from 40% of the compartments in the sanctuary and 38% in MUA, hunting was reported from as many as 35% and 27% of the compartments in the sanctuary and MUA respectively. Although both fishing (4% compartments) and hunting (<1% compartments) were reported from NP, only fishing (12% compartments) was reported from TZ. As far as fishing was concerned, while 12 of the 15 rounds / blocks showed very low intensity fishing pressure, three of the rounds showed low intensity fishing pressure. Very low round-wise hunting pressure was reported from 12 of the rounds. While one round showed low pressure, two of the rounds showed no hunting pressure.

Encroachment

The highest incidence of encroachment was reported from the MUA with 18% of the compartments in the region affected. Encroachment was also reported from the sanctuary area with 11% of the compartments affected. The NP and TZ however, were free of encroachment. A round-wise analysis showed that while 4 of the rounds were free of encroachments, the remaining 11 rounds however, showed very low degree of encroachment.

Relation between various biotic parameters in MTR

Eight pairs of various biotic parameters showed a strong correlation ($r \geq 0.5$) at .01 level of significance (2 tailed) (Table 25). While grazing by domestic livestock showed a very high correlation with fuel collection ($r = 0.720$) and lopping ($r = 0.704$), it also showed a strong correlation with felling ($r = 0.601$) and use of waterholes by domestic livestock ($r = 0.539$). Fuel collection was found strongly correlated to lopping ($r = 0.637$) and felling ($r = 0.679$). It also showed significant correlations to grass cutting ($r = 0.466$) and waterhole use by domestic livestock ($r = 0.419$). While lopping of trees showed a strong correlation to felling ($r = 0.646$), it was also correlated to waterhole use ($r = 0.470$). Fishing and waterhole use by domestic livestock were also found to be correlated ($r = 0.545$).

Linear regression analysis further showed that while grazing was a dependent variable of waterhole usage by livestock ($r^2 = 0.3015$, $p < 0.001$), lopping ($r^2 = 0.4665$, $p < 0.001$), felling ($r^2 = 0.2911$, $p < 0.001$) and fuel collection ($r^2 = 0.7099$, $p < 0.001$) were dependent on grazing. Moreover, fuel collection determined lopping ($r^2 = 0.3353$, $p < 0.001$), felling ($r^2 = 0.421$, $p < 0.001$) and grass cutting ($r^2 = 0.2229$, $p < 0.001$) pressures in MTR.

Table 25: Correlations[1] between various biotic parameters

	Grazing	Fuel collect.	Lopping	Illicit felling	Grass cutting	Encroachment	Hunting	Fishing	Fire
Fuel collect.	0.720** 0.000								
Lopping	0.704** 0.000	0.637** 0.000							
Illicit felling	0.601** 0.000	0.679** 0.000	0.646** 0.000						
Grass cutting	0.346** 0.000	0.466** 0.000	0.379** 0.000	0.387** 0.000					
Encroac-hment	0.208** 0.000	0.261** 0.000	0.207** 0.000	0.284** 0.000	0.116** 0.002				
Hunting	0.176* 0.000	0.117** 0.002	0.253** 0.000	0.285** 0.000	0.086* 0.022	0.144** 0.000			
Fishing	0.377** 0.000	0.337** 0.000	0.375** 0.000	0.377** 0.000	0.193** 0.000	0.155** 0.000	0.358** 0.000		
Fire	0.231** 0.000	0.095* 0.011	0.314** 0.000	0.135** 0.000	0.165** 0.000	0.016 0.668	0.345** 0.000	0.254** 0.000	
Water-hole use	0.539** 0.000	0.419** 0.000	0.470** 0.000	0.382** 0.000	0.303** 0.000	0.146** 0.000	0.184** 0.000	0.545** 0.000	0.280** 0.000

[1] Spearman's rank correlations. ** Correlation is significant at the 0.01 level (2 tailed).* Correlations is significant at the 0.05 level (2 tailed).

Distribution of five major biotic pressure parameters in MTR

The distribution of pressure on account of five of the major biotic parameters, *viz.*, grazing, fuel wood collection, lopping of trees for fodder, illicit felling of trees and grass cutting was assessed both for the different management units and the blocks / rounds. While 75% of the entire tiger reserve area was affected by the major biotic factors, the MUA was the worst affected with all its compartments under pressure, followed by the sanctuary with more than 90% of the area under pressure. The Tourism zone and the NP with 36% and 12% area respectively under pressure were comparatively less affected by these five major biotic factors (Table 26).

Table 26: Distribution of combined biotic pressure* in different management zones / units of Melghat Tiger Reserve

Management zones	Affected		Not affected	
	Area**	Compartments	Area**	Compartments
Melghat Tiger Reserve	1255.30	538 (75.2%)	409.51	177 (24.7%)
Sanctuary	667.78	283 (91.8%)	33.10	25 (8.1%)
Multiple-use area	526.22	227 (100%)	-	-
National Park	41.35	19 (12.25%)	320.13	136 (87.74%)
Tourism Zone	19.64	9 (36%)	36.23	16 (64%)

*The combined pressure of grazing by livestock, fuel wood collection, lopping for fodder, illicit felling of trees and grass cutting was considered for delineating pressure areas. ** Area calculations are square kilometres in GIS domain.*

Table 27: Distribution of combined biotic pressure* in different administrative units of Melghat Tiger Reserve

Rounds	Pressure category
Jarida	6 - very high
Hatru	5 - high
Kuwapati	5 - high

Kolkaz	5 - high
Rangubeli	6 - very high
Harisal	6 - very high
Tarubanda	6 - very high
Kund	4 - moderately high
Chikhaldara	3 - medium
Khongda	1 - very low
Koha	5 - high
Dhakna	4 - moderately high
Dolar	2 - low
Koktoo	3 - medium
Dhargad	4 - moderately high

*The combined pressure of grazing by livestock, fuel wood collection, lopping for fodder, illicit felling of trees and grass cutting was considered for delineating pressure areas.

Although none of the blocks / rounds was completely free of pressure, Jarida, Rangubeli, Harisal and Tarubanda rounds were the worst affected rounds with a very high combined pressure score from all five biotic parameters (Table 27). Khongda and Dolar rounds were comparatively less affected by the combined biotic pressure due to grazing, fuel wood collection, lopping, illicit felling of trees and grass cutting. While Chikhaldara and Koktoo rounds were affected by medium pressure, Kund, Dhakna and Dhargad rounds were affected by moderately high pressure. Eight of the fifteen rounds were affected by high to very high pressure.

As some of the unaffected compartments were found to be outside NP and Tourism zone a compartment-wise assessment was done to identify the reasons for no grazing, lopping, fuel wood collection, illicit felling and grass cutting pressures. Discussions with MTR officials and checking of topo-sheets showed that 18 out of the 25 unaffected compartments were located on steep or hilly terrain, while 7 had a village, cultivation area, road, building or plantations located inside. At the compartment level, while Rangubeli, Harisal and Tarubanda were the worst affected rounds, with none of their compartments free of biotic pressure. The least affected round was however, Khongda with only 11.1% of its compartments under biotic pressure. While 6 out of 19 compartments were affected in Kund round, in Dolar round 10 of its 36 compartments were affected. Moreover, 6 of the rounds, *viz.*, Jarida, Hatru, Kuwapati, Kolkaz, Dhakna and Dhargad had more than 50% of their compartments under pressure from major biotic factors (Tables 28 and 29).

Table 28: Compartment-wise distribution of combined biotic pressure* in different administrative units of Melghat Tiger Reserve

Round	Compartments		
	Total	Affected	Not affected
Jarida	66	63 (95.5%)	3 (4.5%)
Hatru	91	90 (98.9%0	1 (1.1%)
Kuwapati	66	48 (72.7%)	18 (27.3%)
Kolkaz	83	68 (82%)	15 (18%)
Rangubeli	47	47 (100%)	-
Harisal	56	56 (100%)	-
Tarubanda	46	46 (100%)	-
Kund	19	6 (31.6%)	13 (68.4%)
Chikhaldara	36	13 (36.1%)	23 (63.9%)
Khongda	27	3 (11.1%)	24 (88.9%)
Koha	31	15 (48.4%)	16 (51.6%)
Dhakna	43	41 (95.3%)	2 (4.7%)
Dolar	36	10 (27.8%)	26 (72.2%)
Koktoo	41	15 (36.6%)	26 (63.4%)
Dhargad	27	18 (66.7%)	9 (33.3%)

*The combined pressure of grazing by livestock, fuelwood collection, lopping for fodder, illicit felling of trees and grass cutting was considered for delineating pressure areas.

Percentages were calculated over total compartments in a round

Table 29: Characteristics of the unaffected compartments in Melghat Tiger Reserve

Topographic characteristics	Compartment numbers	Total
Steep or hilly terrain (slope >50°)	127, 134, 135, 214 – 218, 243 - 247, 262, 278, 890, 891, 979	18
Village / cultivation / plantation / road / building	172, 173, 175, 181, 263, 280, 286	7

Biotic pressure zones around National Park boundary in MTR

The distribution of combined pressure from grazing, lopping, fuel wood collection, illicit felling of trees and grass cutting was assessed around the National Park boundary. For this 5 km buffers were marked on the combined pressure map and areas under different pressure categories were calculated. In the first 5 km zone around the National Park boundary, 17.5% of the area within MTR boundary was found to be free of pressure. While almost 51% of the area was affected by very low to low pressure, the remaining 31.5% of the area was affected by medium to very high pressure. In the next 5 km zone (between a distance of 5-10 km from the National Park boundary), however, the proportion of the unaffected area increased to 37.5%. The proportionate area under very low to low pressure decreased to around 33%, the area under medium to very high pressure also reduced to around 29%. In the next 5 km buffer (10-15 km from the National Park boundary) however, the percentage of unaffected area reduced drastically to around 16%. The area under low to very low pressure also reduced to 21%, whereas there was a steep rise in area under medium to very high pressure (62% of the total area in this zone).

In the rest of the area beyond 15 km of the National Park boundary, the unaffected area showed a drastic decline whereas the area affected by the combined biotic factors increased (Table 30).

Table 30: Area* under combined biotic pressure around the National Park boundary in Melghat Tiger Reserve

Distance from National Park boundary	Unaffected area (sq.km.)	Affected area (sq.km.)	
		Very low to low pressure (sq.km.)	Medium to very high pressure (sq.km.)
5 km	16.74	48.48	200.00
10 km	38.17	34.24	122.31
15 km	26.53	33.57	98.56
20 km	4.63	47.47	155.60
25 km	4.25	51.45	180.59
30 km	0.00	13.06	114.67
35 km	0.00	0.00	12.44
Total	90.32	228.27	984.96

area calculations are in the GIS domain

Comparison of human, livestock and wildlife densities in MTR

Block-wise human, livestock and wildlife densities were compared. The density figures were recalculated on the area in GIS domain for each round / block. Four wildlife species viz., Gaur, Sambar, Barking deer, and Wild boar, were considered for comparison (Table 31). Gaur was found to be absent in two of the rounds in the MUA (Rounds 1 and 7). It was in very low densities (<1/ sq.km.) in all rounds in northern parts of MTR, mostly falling in the MUA and the sanctuary, except in Hatru round where its density was 2 per square kilometre. Rounds in the southern parts of MTR, i.e., 8, 9, 10, 11, 13, 14 and 15, showed densities of 1 to 3 animals per square kilometre. Thus about 50% of the rounds had 1 to 3 animals per square kilometre.

Sambar densities varied between 1 to 2 animals per square kilometre in all the rounds except 13 and 15, which had 3 and 4 animals per square kilometre respectively. Barking deer however, showed a similar distribution pattern to gaur in the northern rounds, i.e., less than 1 animal per square kilometre, except in Hatru round, which had 1 animal per square kilometre. Moreover, rounds in the southern parts of MTR, i.e., 8, 10, 11, 12, 14 and 15 also had low barking deer densities (<1 per sq.km.), except rounds 9 and 13 which had 1 animal per square kilometre. As far as the wild boar was concerned, except for rounds 3, 14 and 15, which had densities of 3, 2 and 6 per square kilometre respectively, all other rounds had 1 or less than 1 animal per square kilometre. Thus on an average, while sambar and wild boar densities were more than one animal per square kilometre in the entire MTR, gaur and barking deer were found in very low densities of less than one per square kilometre.

Table 31: Round-wise densities of Gaur, Sambar, Barking deer and Wild boar in Melghat Tiger Reserve

Round	Area*	Densities based on 1996 block counts			
		Gaur	Sambar	Barking deer	Wild boar
Jarida	140.42	-	1.17	0.73	1.46
Hatru	195.81	1.86	2.01	0.97	1.19
Kuwapati	152.78	0.08	0.86	0.43	3.01
Kolkaz	184.12	0.22	1.03	0.07	0.29
Rangubeli	111.28	0.36	0.74	0.53	1.61
Harisal	129.71	0.59	1.26	0.59	1.11
Tarubanda	112.04	-	0.78	0.58	0.77
Kund	41.94	0.90	1.57	0.76	0.59

Chikhaldara	88.78	0.96	1.86	1.12	0.21
Khongda	59.93	1.32	0.80	0.28	1.25
Koha	71.65	1.59	1.59	0.80	1.29
Dhakna	112.76	0.07	0.95	0.21	-
Dolar	87.33	1.73	2.97	0.95	1.41
Koktoo	103.86	2.76	2.23	0.56	2.32
Dhargad	72.34	2.76	4.38	0.85	6.02
Average		0.90	1.46	0.60	1.42

Square kilometers in GIS domain.

Human and livestock densities were highest for Tarubanda round, i.e., 30.6 and 26.0 per square kilometer respectively (Table 32). While human density was the lowest in Dolar round (1.79 / sq.km.) the livestock density was lowest in Koktoo round (2.98 / sq.km.). Kund and Khongda rounds however had no people or livestock residing. While six of the rounds had human density of less than 10 people per square kilometre, three of the rounds had 10 - 20 people per square kilometre, and four of the rounds had more than 20 people per square kilometre. As far as the livestock densities were concerned, five of the rounds had less than 10 animals per square kilometre, four of the rounds had 10 - 20 animals per square kilometre and four of the rounds had more than 20 animals per square kilometre.

Table 32: Round-wise human and livestock densities in Melghat Tiger Reserve

Round	Area*	Human densities (1991)	Livestock densities (1993)
Jarida	140.42	28.4	22.7
Hatru	195.81	20.7	24.6
Kuwapati	152.78	4.4	4.3
Kolkaz	184.12	12.3	11.5
Rangubeli	111.28	7.6	10.6
Harisal	129.71	21.9	18.7
Tarubanda	112.04	30.6	26.0

Kund	41.94	-	-
Chikhaldara	88.78	5.5	8.6
Khongda	59.93	-	-
Koha	71.65	4.1	7.6
Dhakna	112.76	15.2	26.3
Dolar	87.33	1.7	3.4
Koktoo	103.86	4.9	2.9
Dhargad	72.34	13.1	14.5
Average			

Square kilometers in GIS domain.

Table 33: Available area and actual round-wise human and livestock densities in Melghat Tiger Reserve

Round	Area inside National Park	Area available	Actual human densities**	Actual livestock densities***
Jarida	0	140.42	28.4	22.7
Hatru	0	195.81	20.7	24.6
Kuwapati	0	152.78	4.4	4.3
Kolkaz	0	184.12	12.3	11.5
Rangubeli	0	111.28	7.6	10.62
Harisal	0	129.71	21.9	18.74
Tarubanda	0	112.04	30.6	26.0
Kund	28.99	12.95	-	-
Chikhaldara	65.62	23.16	21.3	33.2
Khongda	59.95	59.93	-	-
Koha	40.51	31.14	9.5	15.4
Dhakna	0	112.76	15.2	26.3
Dolar	67.75	19.58	8.0	10.6
Koktoo	74.82	29.04	17.5	10.6
Dhargad	24.05	48.29	19.6	21.7

*Square kilometers in GIS domain. ** per square kilometer densities calculated on1991 population census. *** per square kilometer densities calculated on1993 livestock census.*

Seven of the 15 rounds i.e., Kund, Chikhaldara, Khongda, Koha, Dolar, Koktoo and Dhargad, had parts of their area inside the NP boundary. These areas were therefore not available for biotic use, resulting in increasing the actual human and livestock densities in these rounds (Table 33). Two of the rounds, i.e., Kund and Khongda did not have any people or livestock residing within, and were therefore unaffected.

Actual human and livestock densities in the remaining five rounds increased sharply as a result of the decrease in available area. The number of rounds with a human density of 10 - 20 people per square kilometre increased to 4 and those with more than 20 people per square kilometre increased to 5. As far as the livestock densities were concerned, number of rounds with less than 10 animals per square kilometre reduced to one, those with 10 - 20 animals per square kilometre increased to 6 and number of rounds with more than 20 animals per square kilometre increased to 5. Thus overall the actual densities and consequent dependence on these rounds was more than perceived.

Discussion

The national park was mostly free of biotic pressures except on its periphery from 6 villages located very close to the NP boundary. At places the pressure was also reported from compartments within the NP boundary. This was also because of the adjacent villages. However, some compartments located adjacent to compartments with very high or high pressure on the NP boundary, were found free of pressure. It was because of the rugged terrain along most of the NP boundary. Outside the NP, however, pressure from biotic activities was tremendous. Although no biotic activities like grazing, lopping, fuel collection, use of waterholes for livestock, grass cutting, etc., were allowed within the tourism zone, some of the compartments on its boundary were under pressure, primarily from the villages lying close to this zone. Both the sanctuary and multiple-use area were under pressure from various biotic activities. Although, grazing by resident livestock was the major biotic factor affecting these areas some of the compartments were found free of pressure. These were either along rugged terrain, with the slopes being very steep, making it impossible for the livestock to graze or they were in or adjacent to the village areas which were already degraded and there was no fodder available for the livestock. Fuel wood collection also usually does not take place in the immediate vicinity of the villages as was observed by the researcher during her field work. At the administrative level, while 2 of the rounds did not have any villages located within they were also subjected to varying degrees of biotic pressure from villages in adjacent rounds/blocks. Khongda block in the south of MTR, was subjected only to low intensity pressure due to fuelwood collection and grass cutting from adjacent villages especially, Koha which is situated very close to the northern boundary of the NP. Kund block, which was also free of human habitation, was under medium to moderately high grazing and lopping pressure respectively from Kund village which had a livestock population of more than 250 animals.

A strong correlation was found between grazing and use of waterholes by domestic livestock. Grazing was therefore, usually found to be taking place in and around the compartments with waterholes as it was convenient for the graziers especially the agro-pastoralists to take the livestock to these waterholes for watering. Moreover, some of the livestock belonging to the agro-pastoralists illegally camped in the forest close to the waterholes, thus the strong correlation. Grazing also showed a strong correlation to lopping and illicit felling especially in areas which were away from the villages, as the graziers / agro-pastoralists accompanying the livestock usually lopped and sometimes even fell trees for the accompanying cattle to feed on. Moreover, since branches were lopped for fodder for the livestock camping at and close to waterholes, a strong correlation was found between use of waterholes and lopping. Fuel wood collection was also taking place in similar areas as grazing, although comparatively closer to the villages. Although fire did not show a strong correlation with grazing or grass cutting, but it was found to be significantly correlated thus, strengthening the speculation that fires are usually set by the local agro-pastoralists in the belief that it would bring out a fresh flush of grasses.

While most of the rounds in the north and north-west of MTR were under high to very high biotic pressure, majority of the rounds in the lower southern half of MTR were under moderate to low intensity pressure. While majority of the areas in a zone of 5 km around the NP boundary was affected by biotic activities, the unaffected areas marginally increased in the next 5-km zone. However, after that the unaffected area registered a steep decline, as the biotic pressure in the northern MTR was much greater due to the high human and livestock populations especially in the MUA.

Hatru round, which was located in northern MTR, had human and livestock densities of more than 20 per square kilometre. It also had good wildlife densities of Gaur, Sambar and even Barking deer. Most of the blocks in the centre of MTR however, did not have good wildlife densities despite protection to more than 50 square kilometres under tourism zone. In the southern blocks however, gaur densities were slightly higher. The other 3 wildlife species also showed higher densities despite biotic disturbance due to people's dependence on these forests, as no alternative areas were available and most of the villages in the southern blocks were moreover adjacent to or very close to the NP boundary.

Chapter 7

Protected Area – People Conflicts and Management Implications

Protected area – people conflicts

Melghat Tiger Reserve and Bori Wildlife Sanctuary were created for long term conservation of biodiversity focusing on some of the most endangered mammalian species, such as the tiger and the gaur. A large tribal and non-tribal population has been living in and around these two protected areas and has been exploiting the resources of these forests for their survival since time immemorial. The creation of these two protected areas during the first half of the 1970's had created certain problems leading to conflicts between the local people and the protected area officials, i.e., aspirations of the local people and conservation goals of the protected areas. The main problem confronting the local people was the lack of opportunities and benefits which they had traditionally derived from the area prior to its declaration as protected area. As a result, they had been deprived of the resources they had traditionally depended on. On the other hand, crop raiding by wild herbivores and livestock depredation by wild animals created a conflict not only between the local people and wild animals, but also with the protected area officials.

Moreover, the protected area managers of both MTR and BWLS had to face the problem of hunting of wildlife by the local people using traps and dogs, mostly for domestic consumption. At times the local people also resorted to killing of wild animals, especially the Sambar and Wild pig, by using country made bombs; they also poison the carcasses of livestock to kill the tiger and leopard, in retaliation for the damage caused to their agricultural fields and domestic livestock by these wild animals. The local people also harvest fish illegally by blasting bombs under the water and poisoning the water bodies using agricultural pesticides and insecticides, even though they are permitted to catch fish for domestic consumption, using indigenous methods like nets etc. The dual conflict situation, coupled with the problems stated above, reflected the respondents' perceptions of five major problems and conflicts (Table 34).

Table 34: Major problems and conflicts faced by the respondents in Melghat Tiger Reserve and Bori Wildlife Sanctuary

Problems / Conflicts	Melghat Tiger Reserve			Bori Wildlife Sanctuary	
	A	B	C	A	C
LEO	63.47	85.42	14.29	90.63	81.82
SOF	31.14	47.92	92.86	15.63	18.18
UOL	8.98	22.92	3.57	57.81	90.91
CR	71.85	56.25	28.57	90.63	100
LP	5.39	12.5	7.14	56.25	54.55

LEO=Lack of employment opportunities; SOF=Shortage of fodder; UOL=Unavailability of land; CR=Crop raiding by wild herbivores;

LP=Livestock predation by wild animals; A=Scheduled tribes; B=Scheduled castes and backward classes; and C=Agropastoralists.

The figures are percentages of families in each community group.

Lack of employment opportunities was considered as a major problem by majority of the households (more than 60%) from all the communities, except the agropastoralist families of MTR (less than 15%). The agropastoralists in MTR (more than 90%) felt fodder shortage for their livestock and were resentful for not being allowed to graze in the NP and Tourism Zone of MTR. For the rest of the communities, including the agropastoralists from BWLS, less than 50% considered shortage of fodder as a major problem. More than 57% of both tribal and agropastoralist communities from Bori Wildlife Sanctuary considered land as a major requirement. For the rest of the communities from MTR, especially the tribal and agropastoralists, less than 10% considered unavailability of land as a problem.

Crop damage by wild herbivores was a major conflict for more than 60% of households from all communities in both MTR and BWLS, except the agropastoralist households in MTR (less than 40%). Livestock predation however, was considered a major conflict by more than 50% of the households belonging to both tribal and agropastoralist communities from BWLS as compared to the households from MTR (less than 14%).

The long term survival of a protected area depends to a great extent on the good-will and support of the people living in and around it. Conflicts with local communities have occurred practically throughout the world wherever PAs were created ignoring the local people's social, economic and political aspirations (Lusigi, 1981; Abel and Blaikie, 1986; Carew-Reid, 1990; and Talbot and Olindo, 1990). The problems are exacerbated in developing countries where rapidly growing populations are putting increasing pressure on often fragile ecosystems and the governments do not have the resources to invest in protected areas (Hannah, 1992; Durbin and Ralambo, 1994).

In MTR and BWLS, the five major problems and conflicts that emerged from this study were, i) lack of employment opportunities within the two protected areas, ii) shortage of fodder for livestock, iii) unavailability of land for agriculture, iv) crop-damage by wild herbivores and v) livestock predation by wild animals. Over the years, a rift has been created between the local people and the managers of the two protected areas. Most people held the change in status of these forests to National Park, Sanctuary or Tiger Reserve, as being responsible for their problems.

As stated earlier, people especially those belonging to scheduled tribes, castes and other backward classes were traditionally employed as labour in forestry operations. These operations were however stopped with the passing of legislation against any commercial activity within protected areas. Consequently, majority of the local communities felt deprived of their livelihood due to loss of employment opportunities within the two PAs. The remoteness of the area, especially BWLS, had aggravated the problem further. As a result, quite a few of the families were seasonally disturbed or displaced from their homes as they had to go in search of employment opportunities in towns and urban centres. This period coincided with the slump in employment opportunities in the agricultural sector in the villages within the PAs. Moreover, the few employment opportunities available with the forest department were not a very dependable source of income, due to delayed wage payments.

The agro-pastoralists from MTR were resentful of not being permitted to graze their livestock in the NP and Tourism Zone of MTR, where there was plenty of grass due to absence of grazing by domestic livestock. For other communities it was not such a major problem. One probable reason for this could be the large livestock holdings of the agro-pastoralists in MTR (more than 19 animals per household). However, even though the mean livestock holding for the agro-pastoralists from Bori was higher (23 animals per family), shortage of fodder was considered a problem by less than 20% of the families. This could be because of three reasons, *viz.*, (i) the forests of Melghat were of 'dry deciduous' type (with an annual rainfall of 1000 to 2250 mm), whereas that of Bori were of 'moist deciduous' type (with an annual rainfall of 1200 to 3200 mm). Consequently, most of the grasses and leaves dry earlier in MTR, while in Bori they are available for a longer period; (ii) the total domestic livestock population for MTR was higher (20 animals per sq. km) compared to that of Bori (15 animals per sq. km) causing overgrazing and non-availability of fodder in the areas close to the villages; (iii) while the agropastoralists in Bori also practiced agriculture, majority of them in MTR (64% families) did not own any land. As a result most of them were completely dependent on earnings from livestock for their livelihood. Moreover, they did not have the agricultural byproducts and residue for feeding their livestock. Therefore, these families periodically migrated with their livestock, to areas outside the Reserve in search of fodder and pastures. They usually migrated to areas with large agricultural fields where they could keep their livestock for several months. The landowners allow the livestock to graze on agricultural residue because in return for this they get manure (dung) for their fields. This annual migration caused hardship to the agro-pastoralist families and they held the Project Tiger officials responsible for their problems.

More than 50% of the families from both agricultural and agro-pastoralist families of BWLS, considerd the non-availability or or subsistence agricultural landholdings as a major problem for their survival. Primarily because quite a few families were displaced from the western side of the Sanctuary as the villages in this area have come under the submergence of the backwaters of the Tawa Reservoir. However, no compensation or alternatives were provided to these families, and they had been subsisting without land in the Sanctuary. As a result of this most of them had to either depend on labour employment opportunities within and outside the PA for their sustenance, or rent land or do share-cropping. This pushed them into the vicious 'debt trap'.

Crop damage by wild herbivores was another conflict area for most of the agricultural households, as well as the agropastoralists of BWLS. Most of these families practiced subsistence agriculture and were dependent on its produce for sustenance. However, the agropastoralists of MTR did not perceive it a major problem as quiet a few of them were landless (64% families) and their primary occupation and source of livelihood is dairy farming and its allied activities. Agriculture was only a secondary source of livelihood for most of them. Crop depredation by wild herbivores had been a regular occurrence in villages within and adjacent to forests for a long time and people had lived with this problem for centuries. But in the present scenario they considerd the establishment of the PA and the consequent protection given to the wild animals, as well as the ban on the use of firearms for crop protection, which have resulted in increasing the numbers of wild herbivores.

Livestock predation was considered a major conflict by communities in Bori as compared to those in MTR, although the latter had a far higher number of large predators *viz,* tigers and leopards. Also, the cases of livestock predation were comparatively higher (more than 360 cattle kills per annum) in MTR. However, due to a larger number of Territorial and Project Tiger field staff being posted in the villages, the recording of the cases and the disbursement of the compensation was a speedy process therefore the people were less antagonistic towards the forest department. On the contrary, the casual attitude of the forest staff in BWLS towards recording of cases and disbursing of compensation was a major source of resentment of the local people towards the former.

Management Implications

For efficient management of a protected area it is important to take into consideration the human dimension as well since conservation cannot be successful without taking into consideration the needs and factors of dependence of local communities. On the basis of the field study undertaken in MTR and BWLS, three major management issues that emerged were socio-economic, administrative and protected area-people relationships.

Socio-economic issues

There were three major socio-economic issues facing the PA management of MTR and BWLS: Firstly, employment opportunities, especially for those without land and livestock. These 8% of the families were genuinely dependent on the forest resources for their livelihood. Secondly, grazing by large number of livestock within the PAs and the associated fires; this activity was a major cause for weed proliferation and soil compaction leading to decrease in ground cover and rate of regeneration. Thirdly, fuel wood requirement of the people living within the PAs; in the absence of alternative sources, fuel wood was a major source of energy for the people living within the PAs.

Administrative issues

Apart from the socio-economic issues there were two major administrative issues which came in the way of efficient management of the PAs: One, the inadequate coordination between district administration and the forest department and two, the inadequate training and motivation of the forest staff, especially in terms of people related issues.

Protected area-people relationship

Apart from the socio-economic and administrative issues the PA management also needs to deal with PA-people relationship as this can help to develop a positive attitude towards the PA. In case of MTR and BWLS the managers had to deal with two major aspects; One, conflict (in people's perceptions) with the objectives of conservation. On one hand it was the struggle for day to day survival for subsistence for the socio-economic class dependent on the forest resources and on the other hand it was the unsustainability of this resource-use which was undermining the conservation efforts. Two, the negative attitudes of the people towards the Forest Department due to the crop damage and livestock predation by wild animals; the reality was not appreciated or understood.

Implications for management

Most of the protected areas today are facing a number of problems with respect to the people living within and adjacent to them, their dependence on these forests and their rights. Most of these problems require different management strategies as the protected area policy and management also has its implications for rural development of the local people (Schelhas, 1991 and Brechin *et al.*, 1991). IUCN's World Conservation Strategy (IUCN, 1980) emphasised the concept of joining economic development with conservation ('eco-development') for the better management of PAs. Such a holistic, people friendly and inter-agency approach can contribute to environmental security, higher productivity and the well-being of people (Panwar, 1992).

The issues that emerged from this study had implications for the management of Melghat Tiger Reserve and Bori Wildlife Sanctuary. Therefore the management of MTR and BWLS should ensure the following:

Most importantly, provision of alternatives to the genuinely dependent families, in terms of both alternative resources and sources of income, would reduce the pressure on the forest and make the local forest-based economies sustainable in the long run. Women deserve special attention when providing alternatives, as they spend a major portion of their time in collecting fuel wood and water for the family as well as doing other domestic chores.

Local subsistence communities spend considerable time in collecting fuel wood for meeting their energy requirements, both for cooking and heating purposes. Although dry wood is collected for daily fuel wood requirements, live wood is harvested especially before the monsoons. It was seen that despite prohibitions, local communities continue to harvest wood from the forests mainly because of lack of alternatives. Therefore, efforts should be made to provide readily available and appropriate viable alternatives. The forest department is already thinking and acting in this direction. Moreover, incentives should be given to reduce present level of consumption in addition to better management of the existing and newly created resources.

The forest department along with the local NGOs can introduce fuel-efficient devices and smokeless stoves. This will not only conserve fuel but would also win them the support of the women as it would lessen their ordeal of cooking in dark smoke-filled rooms. Other alternatives can be bio-gas plants, especially for the agro-pastoralist families and others with large livestock holdings.

Alternative sources of income can be generated by providing preferential employment to at least one member of the genuinely dependent families, in any forest related activities, e.g., fire watchers, watchmen, trekkers, nursery and silvicultural works, road-making, etc. Thus, the focus should be to address those who have the least range of sustenance opportunities, i.e., 8% of the families, who are landless and also do not own any livestock.

Also emphasis should be on decreasing the bio-dependence of the local people through alternate non-forest based occupations like poultry farming, pig-rearing, fish ponds and other small-scale enterprises.

Secondly, incentives could be given in the form of - permission to cut grass from Tourism Zone and supply of the cut grass from Gugamal National Park of MTR as a result of management activities during post monsoon period and before the fire season to the livestock owners in MTR; incentives should be given to livestock owners of both the PAs, for adopting both stall feeding and resolving to maintain smaller number of more productive livestock. The animal husbandry department needs to adopt a more people friendly approach so as to be more successful in these remote areas.

Moreover, livestock owners from both protected areas should be encouraged to stall feed their livestock on cut grasses and fodder especially during monsoons and early winter, as this is the period when grazing causes damage to the new seedlings that are coming up. With the help of local participation village zones can be demarcated, especially for the purpose of livestock grazing. This may help in restricting the effects of grazing to the areas around the villages and leaving larger areas of the forest undisturbed. Also, the concept of rotational grazing can be introduced, with the help of local planning and participation.

Relations between parks and their immediate neighbours have always been a major problem everywhere, especially in the tropics, as the local people want to continue to exercise their traditional rights. Allowing local people 'controlled access' to certain resources of the protected areas may be necessary for meeting their critical resource-needs. Moreover, permitting such uses can also build local support for these protected areas (Lehmkuhl *et al.*, 1988 and Schelhas, 1991). Such experiments have been successfully tried in Amboseli National Park, Kenya (Shelton, 1983), Royal Chitwan National Park, Nepal (Shelton, 1983; and Lehmkuhl, *et al.*,1988) and Kosi Tappu Wildlife Reserve, Nepal (Heinen, 1993). Local participation would be more successful in creating social fencing of the forests rather than policing of large areas by a few forest guards.

Thirdly, indigenous and fast growing timber and fodder species could be introduced within village boundaries and on fallow lands as this would eventually take at least some pressure off the forest. Care needs to be taken that non-invading species are selected. The villagers need to be enabled to take proper care of these trees. The villagers need to be independent in this respect. Wherever, private lands are used for planting trees or growing fodder, the owners may be provided site specific suitable incentives to encourage them. While all kinds of available wood were collected by the local people in both MTR and BWLS, there was a preference for fuel-efficient species like *saj, tiwas, dhaora, aonla,* etc. While planting trees for the purpose of fuel wood such preferences may be kept in mind. However, the need is to raise the fuel reserve over 'short time' the native species may not accord with this need. Similarly, while planting fodder species care should be taken to plant those species, that are native and which can supply fodder for greater part of the year. Moreover pasture improvement works should also be taken up, wherever possible.

Fourthly, Forest Department can undertake initiative for providing conservation and vocational education to the local youth and women, through short term training camps. NGOs and media options can play a significant role by spreading the message of conservation and motivating the local people to take up small conservation projects at the village level.

Quite a few of the youth in the villages were found interested in acquiring vocational skills like, tailoring, maintaining automobiles, machinery, electrical repairing, shorthand and typing, etc. However, majority of them lacked financial resources to obtain these skills. The Forest Department may involve NGOs to help deserving and interested candidates in obtaining vocational training so as to eventually help them to be self-sufficient. In the long run it may help to reduce the number of unemployed people who would have otherwise been completely dependent on the forests. Apart from this, women may be provided with the necessary help to take up horticultural activities on a small scale on their own land. The forest department along with NGOs may help the women to take up processing and cooperative marketing of collected NTFPs and other cultivated products, for value- addition.

This will not only provide opportunities for gainful employment to the women, but would also empower them by providing financial security. Besides, this could help the forest department to gain crucial support of the women for any conservation-oriented activities. Such activity ecologically could however raise a concern as such enterprise could lead to excessive collection and local extirpation of the concerned species. A balance needs to be struck.

Fifthly, 'Trust building activities' need to be identified by the Forest Department in consultation with the local people. While taking up these activities, the Forest Department can make the linkages very clear to the people, so that people would be able to understand the forest department's willingness to help them, provided the people were willing to co-operate in the department's conservation efforts. A few examples which were worth mentioning are:

(i) Provision of free health and medical facilities- To quote the example of MTR, where 3 days free medical camps were organised by Mr P. J. Thosre, who was then the Field Director of the Reserve during the period of this study. This was really a big step towards gaining people's trust, as a lot of families living in the villages in MTR mentioned during the interviews, how their family members and neighbours had benefitted from these annual camps. Similarly annual mother and child health camps and immunization programmes may be organised for the benefit of the local population. Also, health squads, especially in BWLS and remote villages in

MTR, should be mobilised during monsoons as these villages are completely cut off during this period.

(ii) Although facilities for primary and secondary education were available in quite a few villages, the management was very poor. Consequently, both the children and the parents felt dissatisfied leading to a high drop-out rate. The Forest Department may take the initiative in ensuring better educational facilities to the village children. This will not only help impart primary education to the people and build their trust in the Forest Department, but also provide employment to the educated youth within the villages. Moreover, forest department could also help the unemployed youth obtain vocational training as part of trust-building measure. All these activities would in the long run help the local youth in being self-sufficient, and would make them less antagonistic towards the Forest and Wildlife officials and more aware of their responsibilities towards conservation.

Sixthly, Forest Department has the potential to play a major role in developing an institutional set up for inter-departmental coordination, across agencies operating in the area, with the former acting as the nodal agency, as they best know what can be beneficial or detrimental to the objectives of conservation. Only it needs to be provided the enabling situation. Here again Melghat had set an example in initiating a workshop in 1995 of all government agencies in the area (e.g., tribal welfare, irrigation, soil and moisture conservation, agriculture) and various local NGOs, to help in developing greater coordination between the departments.

These agencies collectively, under a synergised agenda can help local people to adopt improved and appropriate techniques of dry farming, water harvesting, soil conservation, animal husbandry, agro-forestry, etc., aimed at enhancing their income from on- and off-farm activities, so as to reduce their economic dependence on the forest. Moreover, the local units of the agriculture department may be involved in helping the local farmers to adopt organic farming within the protected areas, by choosing appropriate crops, keeping in mind the size of land, availability of irrigation and the financial constraints. This is a long-term view. A start needs to be made. These agencies need to promote co-operative farming; the marginal and small farmers are of particular concern.

Seventhly, blocks in the southern portion of MTR needed management attention. Efforts should be made to reduce the anthropogenic pressures as these blocks had significant wildlife densities. Moreover, although the pressure in the NP was on the periphery with increasing human and livestock population in these villages and consequently depleting forests, the only alternative to these villagers would be the NP forests. There was no alternative forest available outside MTR as the pressures outside were much higher.

Since significant gaur density was recorded in Hatru round in the MUA, biotic pressures on the round should be reduced and adequate protection be given to the habitat despite the de-notification. The Kuwapati and Kolkaz rounds also needed immediate attention as more than 70% of the area was affected despite only a few villages being located in it and parts of it were under the tourism zone. Further, although Khongda block was mostly free of biotic pressure, the comparatively low wildlife densities in it need to be investigated. Probably it was on account of the existing attributes.

Eighth, appropriate training should be provided to the forest staff to deal with the people living within their jurisdiction so as to help build improved relations between the two, which would lead to better management of the area. Moreover, incentives may be given to the field staff for staying in the remote areas and working in difficult situations. It is easier said than done. The management is competent to resolve this.

Ninth, micro-planning with local participation should be regularly taken up in representative villages of various categories as with changing human population, people's requirements also change. After the initial findings the micro-planning exercise may be followed up in the remaining villages in each category. It is important to ensure representation.

The National Forest Policy of 1988 promotes the concept of forest management with the active participation of the local people. Madhya Pradesh is one of the states, which has adopted collective forest management by forming village forest protection committees (Bahuguna *et al.*, 1994). People's participation in management of forest and its resources has already shown positive results in certain forest divisions of West Bengal and Madhya Pradesh (Malhotra, 1993; Dhar, 1994 and Bahuguna *et al.*, 1994). Although, so far these committees have not been formally formed in villages within wildlife sanctuaries, it is time that necessary steps were taken towards creating awareness and bringing about greater involvement of the local people in the protection of such areas. The most significant difference is that there cannot be usufruct sharing. It has to be off-site and the department is the best judge.

Local communities residing within and adjacent to protected areas, in most of the developing countries of Asia and Africa, depend on these forests for their sustenance. Several studies in both India and Nepal (Moench, 1989; Singh and Singh, 1989; and Heinen, 1993) have focused on local people's dependence on forest resources like fuel wood, NTFPs, timber and fodder / grasses. Although the local people may be permitted to collect some of these resources for domestic use, this dependence will not be sustainable in the long run due to rapid increase in human and livestock populations, wealth disparities and natural calamities like floods and drought which cause large scale damage to the forests. Moench (1989) in his study on the Himalayas has stated that even subsistence-use of forest products such as fuel wood and fodder, can over time degrade the resource-base. So far no intensive studies have been carried out on the sustainability of this resource-use in the protected areas (e.g. sanctuaries and Tiger Reserves) of Central Indian Highlands. Such studies are urgently needed for most of India's protected areas as most of them have people living both within and adjacent to them. The greatest challenge is to define sustainability.

The present study was an attempt to understand the complex relationship between the protected areas of MTR and BWLS and the people living and to a lesser extent around them. It was found that both the tribal as well as non-tribal communities were dependent on the forests of MTR and BWLS for their sustenance. However, this dependence did not appear to be sustainable in the long run due to the growth in population and change in lifestyles of these communities over time. Therefore it is suggested that for better management and long-term conservation of MTR and BWLS the forest department ought to win people's support and co-operation through trust-building activities and educational programmes aimed at convincing people about the need for and benefits of conservation. This needs to be followed up with providing appropriate alternatives and incentives to the local people for reducing their dependence on the forest so as to be able to provide conservation to the rich biodiversity of the region. Moreover, active participation of local governmental and non-governmental bodies in the conservation efforts of the PA managers should be encouraged.

Appendices

I. List of villages in Melghat Tiger Reserve

S. No.	Village names	Human population (1991 census)	Livestock population (1993 census)
1.	Chunkhedi	386	468
2.	Khadimal	609	409
3.	Khandukheda	228	133
4.	Ghana	209	210
5.	Awagarh	372	239
6.	Mehriam	497	580
7.	Jarida	682	227
8.	Kamida	323	167
9.	Barugavhan	506	436
10.	Marita	330	426
11.	Sumita	256	262
12.	Ektai	572	532
13.	Simori	559	679
14.	Chilati	249	249
15.	Ruipathar	219	222

16.	Sarwarkhera	344	525
17.	Hatru	702	785
18.	Kuhi	279	336
19.	Domi	188	331
20.	Bhutrum	356	479
21.	Khokmar	175	250
22.	Khamda	222	112
23.	Kund	135	257
24.	Rangubeli	219	390
25.	Ghokda	104	173
26.	Chaurakund	576	515
27.	Tangada	249	294
28.	Harisal	1352	696
29.	Gadgabhandum	265	224
30.	Sawariya	282	726
31.	Kesarpur	642	533
32.	Chikhali	1165	456
33.	Bhiroja	508	598
34.	Patkhau	161	143
35.	Tarubanda	352	491
36.	Keli	470	622
37.	Raksha	111	240

38.	Bhandum	182	328
39.	Dhabya	233	314
40.	Vairat	116	279
41.	Pastalai	157	98
42.	Churni	113	272
43.	Memna	109	122
44.	Semadoh	1087	969
45.	Pili	388	513
46.	Makhala	795	649
47.	Madizarap	178	323
48.	Raipur	679	670
49.	Chopan	265	387
50.	Malur	404	539
51.	Mangia	549	544
52.	Rora	293	400
53.	Kund	183	331
54.	Koha	296	549
55.	Adhao	341	991
56.	Dhakna	422	388
57.	Gularghat	472	336
58.	Bori	97	161

59.	Dhargad	379	553
60.	Kelpani	509	310
61.	Dolar	157	303

Source: Project Tiger Office, Melghat Tiger Reserve.

II. List of villages in Bori Wildlife Sanctuary

S. No.	Village Names	Human population (1991 census)	Livestock population (1991 census)
1.	Bori	295	NA
2.	Dhain	236	NA
3.	Kakri	95	NA
4.	Churna	308	665
5.	Malini	501	598
6.	Mana	391	481
7.	Sakai	315	421
8.	Sakot	99	630
9.	Khakrapura	96	NA
10.	Suplai	325	606
11.	Jhalai	257	470
12.	Mallupura	120	460
13.	Khamda	213	413
14.	Podar	335	620
15.	Bharbhur	240	296
16.	Jam	205	381
17.	Ratibandar	234	169

Source: Forest Department, Bori Wildlife Sanctuary.

III. Importance Value Indices (IVI) of tree species (GBH ≥30 cm) in disturbed and undisturbed forests of Melghat Tiger Reserve and Bori Wildlife Sanctuary

SPC	DF1				UF				DF2			
	RDEN	RFRQ	RDOM	IVI	RDEN	RFRQ	RDOM	IVI	RDEN	RFRQ	RDOM	IVI
1	0.61	1.60	0.27	2.49					1.45	1.69	0.61	3.75
3	0.92	1.83	3.57	6.32	1.40	2.78	3.16	7.34	0.29	0.56	0.95	1.80
4	0.53	0.92	0.48	1.93					1.16	2.26	0.50	3.92
5	0.08	0.23	0.22	0.53								
6	0.08	0.23	0.19	0.49	0.16	0.35	0.07	0.57	0.58	1.13	0.11	1.82
7	2.36	5.03	2.19	9.59	1.71	3.47	2.05	7.23	1.45	2.82	0.70	4.97
9					0.47	1.04	0.54	2.04				
10	0.08	0.23	0.17	0.48	0.16	0.53	0.11	0.61				

11	0.38	0.92	0.11	1.41					1.45	1.69	0.57	3.68
12	1.83	3.20	3.88	8.91	0.62	1.39	0.99	3.0				
13	0.38	1.14	0.24	1.77	0.93	1.39	0.95	3.27	0.87	1.13	1.27	3.27
14	0.46	1.14	0.31	1.91	1.09	2.08	1.64	4.81	1.16	1.13	0.24	2.52
15	2.06	3.20	2.99	8.25	0.62	0.69	0.56	1.88	2.60	3.95	1.90	8.46
16	0.08	0.23	0.05	0.36								
17	0.46	1.14	0.22	1.82	0.47	0.69	0.46	1.62	0.29	0.56	0.12	0.98
19	1.37	2.52	0.62	4.51	0.31	0.69	0.29	1.29				
20	0.46	1.14	0.13	1.73	0.78	1.74	0.18	2.69	0.29	0.56	0.14	1.00
21									6.07	5.08	2.27	13.42
23	0.08	0.23	0.05	0.35	0.78	1.74	1.74	4.26	1.45	2.26	1.45	5.15
25									0.58	1.13	0.12	1.82

26	21.57	4.40	7.34	9.83	1.24	0.23	0.69	0.31	2.37	0.31	1.14	0.92
27	8.06	1.19	2.82	4.05	5.46	0.81	2.78	1.87	6.55	1.06	3.89	1.60
28					0.55	0.05	0.35	0.16	1.11	0.20	0.69	0.23
29	0.89	0.04	0.56	0.29					0.46	0.15	0.23	0.08
30	1.22	0.08	0.56	0.58								
33	2.84	0.28	1.69	0.87	0.54	0.04	0.35	0.16	1.71	0.19	1.14	0.38
34	2.92	0.62	0.56	1.73								
35	1.89	0.18	1.13	0.58								
36					13.46	6.25	3.47	3.74	0.97	0.36	0.46	0.15
38	4.41	0.42	2.26	1.73	10.80	1.63	5.90	3.27	1.40	0.40	0.69	0.31
41					1.65	0.17	0.69	0.78				
42	1.24	0.09	0.56	0.58	6.18	0.84	3.47	1.87	1.06	0.15	0.69	0.23

43	3.89	8.01	2.91	14.81	5.30	7.29	3.13	15.72	2.31	3.95	0.70	6.97
44	1.14	2.52	1.18	4.84	0.93	1.74	0.91	3.58	4.62	5.65	2.28	12.55
45	0.69	0.92	3.01	4.61	1.25	1.74	1.98	4.96	4.62	5.65	6.47	16.74
47	0.92	2.29	1.91	5.11	0.93	1.74	1.63	4.30	1.45	2.26	0.46	4.17
48												
49	4.42	5.26	2.41	12.10	9.50	9.72	6.02	25.25	0.58	1.13	0.52	2.22
51	0.08	0.23	0.05	0.35	1.40	1.74	0.59	3.73				
52	0.23	0.46	0.09	0.78					0.87	1.69	0.14	2.70
53	0.38	1.14	0.28	1.80	0.93	2.08	0.43	3.45	2.89	3.95	1.31	8.15
54					0.31	0.69	0.25	1.25				
55	0.15	0.46	0.46	1.07	0.47	1.04	0.38	1.89	0.58	0.56	2.4	3.56
56	0.69	0.92	0.89	2.50	0.47	1.04	0.47	1.98				

58	0.23	0.46	0.10	0.79	0.16	0.35	0.23	0.73				
59	0.08	0.23	0.02	0.33								
60	0.08	0.23	0.01	0.32	0.47	1.04	0.49	2.0	0.87	1.13	0.24	2.24
61					0.16	0.35	0.60	1.10				
62					0.31	0.69	0.15	1.16				
63	0.53	0.69	1.43	2.65					1.16	1.69	0.29	3.14
65	62.47	27.0	56.93	146.41	47.35	20.14	52.79	120.28	21.68	9.04	52.59	83.30
66									0.58	1.13	1.69	3.40
67	0.23	0.46	0.53	1.21	0.31	0.69	0.55	1.55	0.29	0.56	0.08	0.93
68	0.31	0.92	0.44	1.66								
69	4.50	7.78	7.25	19.53	2.49	5.21	4.30	12.0	9.25	10.17	10.84	30.26
71	1.07	1.37	0.70	3.14	0.16	0.35	0.10	0.61	0.29	0.56	0.04	0.89

SPC												
72	0.38	0.69	0.35	1.42								15.03
74	0.84	2.29	0.35	3.47	5.45	6.25	2.24	13.94	7.23	6.21	1.59	15.03

SPC=Species codes; GBH=Girth at breast height; DF1=Disturbed forest of Melghat Tiger Reserve; UF=Undisturbed forest of Gugamal National Park and Tourism Zone of Melgha t Tiger Reserve; DF2=Disturbed forest of Bori Wildlife Sanctuary; RDEN=Relative density; RFREQ=Relative frequency; RDOM=Relative dominance; and IVI=Importance Value Index.

IV. Scientific and common names of tree species found in disturbed and undisturbed forests of Melghat Tiger Reserve Bori Wildlife Sanctuary

SPC	Scientific Names	Local Names
1	*Acacia catechu*	Khair
2	*Acacia leucopholia*	Rinjha, Reunja
3	*Adina cordifolia*	Haldu, Hardu
4	*Aegle marmelos*	Bel
5	*Ailanthus excelsa*	Maharukh
6	*Albizzia odoratissim*	Chichola
7	*Anogeissus latifolia*	Dhaora
8	*Antidesma diandrum*	Amta, Khatpan
9	*Bauhinia malabarika*	Chaapa, Asthura
10	*Bauhinia purpurea*	Koylari, Keolari
11	*Bauhinia racemosa*	Apta, Astara
12	*Boswellia serrata*	Salai
13	*Bridellia retusa*	Karkha, Kassai
14	*Buchanania latifolia*	Chironji, Achar
15	*Butea monosperma*	Palas
16	*Capparis zeylanica*	Pachwa
17	*Careya arborea*	Kumbhi
18	*Casearia elliptica*	Kesa, Bheri, Tondri
19	*Casearia graveolens*	Riwit, Girchi

SPC	Scientific Names	Local Names
20	*Casia fistula*	Amaltas
21	*Chloroxylon swieteniodes*	Bhirra, Ghiria
22	*Cordia dichotoma*	Bhokar, Silu, Labora
23	*Dalbergia paniculata*	Phasi, Dhoben
24	*Dalbergia sissoo*	Shishu, sissoo
25	*Desmodium pulohollum*	Parpata
26	*Diospyros melanoxylon*	Tendu
27	*Emblica officinalis*	Aonla
28	*Eleodendron glaucum*	Jhamras, Jamrassi
29	*Ficus glomerata*	Gular, Umar
30	*Ficus hispida*	Katumbar, Kareelaumar
31	*Ficus infectoria*	Pakar, Phephar
32	*Ficus religiosa*	Pipal
33	*Flaucortia indica*	Gurguti, Kakai
34	*Gardenia latifolia*	Ghogar, Papra
35	*Gardenia turgida*	Phetra, Phendra
36	*Garuga pinnata*	Kekad, Kakad
37	*Gmelina arborea*	Kasamar, Sewan
38	*Grewia Tiliefolia*	Dhaman
39	*Helicteres isora*	Maror phali
40	*Holarrhena antidysentrica*	Kurkutoo, Dudhi

SPC	Scientific Names	Local Names
41	*Ixora arborea*	Lokhandi
42	*Kydia calycina*	Arang, Baranga
43	*Lagerstroemia parviflora*	Lendia
44	*Lannea coromandelica*	Moyen, Gunja
45	*Madhuca indica*	Mahua
46	*Mangifera indica*	Amba, Aam
47	*Mitragyna parviflora*	Kalam, Kaim
48	*Nyctanthes arbortristis*	Keolari, Karsali
49	*Ougeinia oojeinensis*	Tinsa, Tiwas
50	*Pongamia pinnata*	Karanjalan, Karanji
51	*Pterocarpus marsupium*	Bija
52	*Randia dumetorum*	Bhitu, Menar
53	*Saccopetalum tomentosum*	Humba, Karu
54	*Salmalia malabaricum*	Semal
55	*Schleichera oleosa*	Kusum, Baru
56	*Schrebera swietenioides*	Mokha
57	*Securinega virosa*	Pithondi
58	*Semecarpus anacardium*	Biba, Bhilma
59	*Sesbania sesban*	Saori
60	*Soymida febrifuga*	Rohan, Rohini
61	*Sterculia urens*	Karai, Kulu

SPC	Scientific Names	Local Names
62	*Stereospermum personatum*	Padar
63	*Syzygium cumini*	Jamun
64	*Tamarindus indica*	Chinch, Imli
65	*T ectona grandis*	Sagun, Sagwan
66	*Terminalia arjuna*	Arjun, Kahu
67	*Terminalia bellirica*	Beheda, Behera
68	*Terminalia chebula*	Hirda, Harra
69	*Terminalia tomentosa*	Saj
70	*Vitex negundo*	Sameli, Nirgur
71	*Wrightia tinctoria*	Dudhai, Dudhi
72	*Zizyphus muritiana*	Bor, Ber
73	*Zizyphus rugosa*	Churni, churna
74	*Zizyphus xylopyrus*	Ghatbhor, Ghatol

SPC=Species Codes; GBH=Girth at breast height.

V. Protected area-people: Problems and conflicts in Melghat Tiger Reserve and Bori Wildlife Sanctuary*

Problems/ Conflicts	Melghat Tiger Reserve			Bori Wildlife Sanctuary	
	A	B	C	A	C
LEO	63.47	85.42	14.29	90.63	81.82
FWS	11.38	22.92	3.57	-	-
SOF	31.14	47.92	92.86	15.63	18.18
LPCD	71.25	62.50	39.29	85.94	90.91
UOL	8.98	22.92	3.57	57.81	90.91
LDP	71.86	68.75	35.71	51.56	36.36
LDL	56.87	54.17	53.57	43.75	9.09
LIF	77.25	54.17	35.71	78.13	90.91
LMF	25.75	33.33	28.57	89.06	100.00
IR	11.98	25.00	7.14	76.56	90.91
LVS	22.75	31.25	50.00	87.50	100.00
LEF	3.59	10.42	7.14	1.56	-
SOT	25.15	41.67	14.29	3.13	-
LDF	0.59	-	-	-	-
UOE	22.75	27.08	25.00	7.81	-
CR	71.85	56.25	28.57	90.63	100.00
LP	5.39	12.50	7.14	56.25	54.55

Figures are in percentages. LEO=Lack of employment opportunities; FWS=Fuelwood shortage; SOF=Shortage of fodder; LPCR=Lack of protection from crop depredation; UOL=Unavailability of land; LDP=Lack of drinking water for people; LDL=Lack of drinking water for livestock; LIF=Lack of irrigation facilities; LMF=Lack of medical facilities; IR=Improper roads; LVS=Lack of veterinary services; LEF=Lack of education facilities; SOT=Shortage of timber for domestic purposes; LDF=Lack of dairy facilities; UOE=Unavailability of electricity; CR=Crop raiding by wild herbivores; LP=Livestock predation by wild animals.

References

Abel, N. and Blaike, P. (1986). Elephants, people, parks and development: the case of Luangwa Valley, Zambia. *Environmental Management,* 10, pp. 735-51.

Adhikari, A. D. (1988). Fuelwood use and deforestation in Nepal. Pp. 395-9. In Ramani, K. V. (Ed.)(1989). *Rural Energy Planning: Asian and Pacific Experiences.* Asian and Pacific Development Centre, Kaula Lumpur, Malaysia.

Anderson, D. and Grove, R. (Eds.)(1987). *Conservation in Africa.* Cambridge University Press, UK.

Anon. (1972). *Wildlife Protection Act.* Ministry of Environment and Forests. Government of India, New Delhi, India.

APROSC (1983). *A Feasibility Study on the Provision of Fuelwood for Urban Areas, Nepal,* Vol. II. A report submitted to the Department of Forestry, Kathmandu, Nepal.

Azra, B. (2012) *Environment and Forest Management in India.* Unpublished Ph.D. Thesis. Department of Economics, Aligarh Muslim University, Aligarh.

Bahuguna, V. K., Luthra, V. and Rathor, B. M. S. (1994). Collective forest management in India. *Ambio*, 23, pp. 269-73.

Bajracharya, D. (1983). Fuel, food or forest: Dilemmas in a Nepali village. *World Development*, 11, pp. 1057-74.

Barbier, E. B. (1987). The concept of sustainable economic development. *Environmental Conservation*, 14, pp. 101-10.

Basu, A. (1970). Anthropometry of the Korkus of the Melght forest. *Man in India,* 52, pp. 73-81.

Béteille, A. and Madan, T. N. (Eds.)(1975). *Encounter and Experience:Personal Accounts of Fieldwork*. Vikas Publishing House Private Limited, Delhi, India.

Blaikie, P. (1985). *The Political Economy of Soil Erosion in Developing countries.* Longman, New York, NY, USA.

Blower, J. (1984). Terrestrial Parks for Developing Countries. Pp. 722-7. In McNeely, J. A. and Miller, K. R. (Eds).

Bourliere, F. (Ed.)(1983). *Ecosystems of the World 13, Tropical Savannas*. Elsevier, Amsterdam.

Bowonder, B., Prasad, S. S. R. and Unni, N. V. M. (1987). Deforestation around urban centres in India. *Environmental Conservation*, 14, pp. 23-28.

Brechin, S. R., West, P. C., Harmon, D. and Kutay, K. (1991). Resident Peoples and Protected Areas: A Framework for Enquiry. Pp. 5-28. In West, P. C. and Brechin S. R. (Eds).

Brower, D. J. and Carol D. S. (Eds.)(1987). *Managing Land-Use Conflicts: Case Studies in Special Area Management*. Duke University Press, Durham, UK.

Bunting, B. W. and Sherpa, M. N. (1991). Annapurna Conservation Area: Nepal's New Approach to Protected Area Management. Pp. 160-72. In West, P. C. and Brechin S. R. (Eds).

Burton (1951). Wildlife reserves in India: Uttar Pradesh. *Journal of Bombay Natural History Society*, 49, pp. 749-54.

Calhoun, J. B. (1972). Plight of the Ik and Kaiadilt is seen as a chilling possible end for Man. *Smithsonian*, 3, pp. 26-33.

Carew-Reid, J. (1990). Conservation and protected areas on South-Pacific islands: the importance of tradition. *Environmental Conservation*, 17, pp. 29-38.

Champion, H. G. and Seth, S. K. (1968). *A Revised Survey of the Forest Types of India*. Manager of Publication, New Delhi, India.

Chattopadhyay, K. P. (1941). Korku physical type and the racial affinities. *Journal of Royal Asiatic Society (Bengal)*, 18(1).

Clark, W. C. and Munn, R. E. (Eds.)(1986). *Sustainable Development of the Biosphere*. Cambridge University Press, Cambridge, England, UK.

Cohn, B. S. (1961). Chamar family in a North Indian village; a structural conttingent. *Economic Weekly*, 13, pp. 1051-55.

Croft, T. A. (1981). Lake Malawi National Park: a case study in conservation planning. *Parks*, 6, pp. 7-11.

Dasmann, R.F., Milton, J. P. and Freeman, P. (1973). *Ecological Principles for Economic Development*. John Wiley and Sons, London, England, U.K.

Davis, S. H. (1977). *Victims of the Miracle: Development and the Indians of Brazil.* Cambridge University Press, Cambridge, UK.

deBlohm, C. (1992). Joint efforts for the conservation of Cuare Wildlife Refuge, Venezuela. *Parks*, 3, pp. 14-17.

Desai, I. P. (1955). 'An analysis' in 'Symposium on Caste and Joint Family', *Sociological Bulletin,* 4, pp. 97-117.

Dhar, S. K. (1994). Rehabilitation of degraded tropical forest watersheds with people's participation. *Ambio*, 23, pp. 216-21.

Dhore, M. A. and Joshi, P. A. (1988). *Flora of Melghat Tiger Reserve*. Technical Series No. 1, Directorate of Project Tiger Melghat, Parathwada, India.

Dixon, J. and Sherman, P. (1990). *Economics of Protected Areas: A New Look at Benefits and Costs.* East West Centre, Washington D.C., USA.

Durbin, J. C. and Ralambo, J. A. (1994). The role of local people in the successful maintenance of protected areas in Madagascar. *Environmental Conservation*, 21, pp. 115-20.

Durkheiem, E. (1976). *The Elementary Forms of Religious Life*. George Allen and Unwin, London, UK.

Eckholm, E. A., Foley, G., Barnard, G. and Timberlake, L. (1984). *Fuelwood: The Energy Crisis That Won't Go Away*. International Institute for Environment and Development, London, UK.

Eidsvik,, H. K. (1980). National parks and other protected areas: some reflections on the past and prescriptions for the future. *Environmental Conservation*, 7, pp. 185-90.

Erickholm, E.P. (1975). The deterioration of mountain environments. *Science*, 189, pp. 764-70.

FAO. (1981 a). *Production Year Book*. FAO, Rome.

FAO. (1981 b). *Agriculture: Toward 2000*. FAO, Rome.

FAO. (1984). *Framework for Review of Forest Policy of Ministry of Lands, Natural Resources and Tourism*. Tanzania Government.

Farmer, B. H. (1974). *Agricultural Colonization in India Since Independence*. Oxford University Press, New York, NY, USA.

Fenerstein, M., Shaw, A. and Lovel, H. (1987). The role of livestock in community development. *Community Development Journal*, 22, pp. 174-88.

Fernandes, W., Menon, G. and Viegas, P. (1988). *Forests, Environment and Tribal Economy: Deforestation, Impoverishment and Marginalisation in Orissa*. Tribes of India Series: 2. Indian Social Institute, New Delhi, India.

Firth, R. (1956). *Human Types: An Introduction to Social Anthropology*. Thomas Nelson and Sons Ltd., London, UK.

Forester, R. (1973). *Planning for Man and Nature in National Parks: Reconciling Perpetuation and Use*. IUCN Publication No. 26, IUCN, Gland, Switzerland.

Forsyth, J. (1889). *The Highlands of Central India: Notes on Their forests and Wild Tribes, Natural History and Sports*. London, Chapman and Hall, UK.

Fox, J. (1983). *Managing Public Lands in a Subsistence Economy: the Perspective From a Nepali Village*. Ph.D thesis, University of Wisconsin, Madison, Wisconsin, USA.

Fuchs, S. (1972). Anthropometric analysis of the Korkus and Nahals in the Melghat. *Man in India,* (Ranchi), 52, pp. 73-81.

Fuchs, S. (1988). *The Korkus of the Vindhya Hills*. Tribal Studies of India Series: T124. International-India Publications, New Delhi, India: Pp. 443.

Gadgil, M. (1985). Cultural evolution of ecological prudence. *Landscape Planning*, 12, pp. 285-99.

Gogate, M. G. (1992). Harmonization of grazing needs of domestic herbivora with wildlife management goals. Pp.

149-52 in GOGATE, THOSARE and BANUBAKODE (Eds.).

Gogate, M. G., Thosare, P. J. and Banubakode, S. B. (Eds.) (1992). *Two Decades of Project Tiger, Melghat: Past, Present, Future- 1973-1993*. Papers and Proceedings, October 1-3, 1992. Melghat Project Tiger, Parathwada, India.

Gogate, M. G. (1988). *Management Plan for Melghat Tiger Reserve, 1988-98*. Directorate of Project Tiger Melghat, Parathwada, India.

GOI. (1976). *Report of the National Commission on Agriculture, Part IX, Forestry*. Ministry of Agriculture and Irrigation. New Delhi, India.

GOI. (1982). *Report of the Committee on Forests and Tribals in India*. Ministry of Home Affairs, Tribal Development Division. New Delhi, India.

Goode, W. J. and Hatt, P. K. (1954). *Methods in Social Research*. McGraw Hill Book Company Inc., New York, USA.

Goodland, R. J. A. and Irwin, H. S. (1975). *Amazon Jungle: Green Hell to Red Desert?* Elsevier, Amsterdam, Netherlands.

Greig-Smith, P. (1983). *Quantitative plant ecology*. University of California Press, Berkley, California.

Guha, R. (Ed.)(1994). *Social Ecology*. Oxford University Press, Delhi, India.

Guha, R. (2005). *The Unquiet Woods: Ecological Change and Peasant Resistance in the Himalaya.* In *The Ramachandra Guha Omnibus.* Oxford University Press, New Delhi.

Guppy, N. G. L. (1980). Some crucial issues of our time. *Environmental Conservation,* 7, pp. 3-8.

Gupta, I. and Guleria, A. (1992). *Non-Wood Forest Products in India:Economic Potentials.* CMA Monograph No. 87. Oxford and IBH Publishing Co., New Delhi, India.

Haimendorf, C. von Furer.(1982). *Tribes of India: The Struggle for Survival.* Oxford University Press, Delhi, India.

Hannah, L. (1992). *African People, African Parks.* Conservation International, Washington, D.C., USA.

Hardin, G. (1968). The tragedy of the commons. *Science,* 162, pp. 1243-8.

Hart, W. J. (1966). *A Systems Approach to Park Planning.* IUCN, Morges, Switzerland.

Heinen, J.T. (1993). Park-people relations in Kosi Tappu Wildlife Reserve, Nepal: a socio-economic analysis. *Environmental Conservation,* 20, pp. 25-34.

Hjort, A. (1982). A critique of 'ecological' models of land use. *Nomadic Peoples,* 10, pp. 11-27.

Homewood, K. and W. A. Rodgers (1987). Pastoralism, conservation and the overgrazing controversy. Pp. 111-28 in ANDERSON and GROVE (Eds.).

Hora, S. L. (1937 a). Geographical distribution of Indian fresh water fishes and its bearing on the probable land connections between India and adjacent countries. *Current Science*, 5, pp. 351-56.

Hora, S. L. (1937 b). Distribution of Himalayan fishes and its bearing on certain paleogeographical problems. *Rec. Indian Mus.*, 39, pp. 251-59.

Hough, J.L. (1988). Obstacles to effective management of conflicts between national parks and surrounding human communities in developing countries. *Environmental Conser*vation, 15, pp. 129-36.

Hudson, N. W. (1980). Social, political and economic aspects of soil conservation. Pp.45-54 in MORGAN (Ed.).

Ishwaran, N. and Erdelen, W. (1990). Conserving Sunharaja- an experiment in sustainable development in Sri Lanka. *Ambio*, 12, pp. 237-44, illustr.

IUCN. (1984). *National Conservation Strategies: A Framework for Sustainable development*. IUCN Gland, Switzerland.

IUCN's Commission on Ecology (1980). *World Conservation Strategy: Living Resource Conservation for Sustainable development*: IUCN-UNEP-WWF, Gland, Switzerland.

Kaul, R. N. and Gurumurti, K. (1981). Forest energy in India: the state of the art. *Indian Forester*, 107, pp. 737-43.

Keel, S., Gentry, A. H. and Spinzi, L. (1993). Using vegetation analysis to facilitate the selection of conservation sites in Eastern Paraguay. *Conservation Biology*, pp. 66-75.

Kelly, R. and Walker, B. (1976). The effects of different forms of land use on   the ecology of a semi-arid region in south-western Rhodesia. *Journal of Ecology*, 64, pp. 553-76.

Kennedy, J. (1991). *Ecology of Human Settlements in some tribal villages in Kodaikanal with special emphasis on MFPs, Agroecosystems and Domestic Sector.* SAS Ecology, M.Sc. Dissertation.

Kiss, A. (Ed.)(1990). *Living with Wildlife: Wildlife Resource Management with Local Participation in Africa.* World Bank Technical Paper 130, World Bank, Washington, D.C., USA.

Knight, D. H. (1975). A phytosociological analysis of species-rich tropical forest on Barro Colorado Island, Panama. *Ecological Monograph* 45, pp. 259-84.

Kolenda, P. M. (1968). Region, caste and family structure: a comparative study   of the Indian "joint" family. Pp. 339-96 in SINGER and COHN (Eds.).

Kumar, M. S. (Ed.)(1987). *Energy Pricing Policies in Developing Countries:Theory and Empirical Evidence.* UNDP/ESCAP, Bangkok, Thailand.

Ladkat, N. S. and Chopkar, R. D. (1993). People of Melghat. Pp. 91-5 in GOGATE, THOSARE and BANUBAKODE (Eds.).

Lal, J. B. (1989). *India's Forests, Myth and Reality.* Natraj Publishers, Dehra Dun, India.

Lamprey, H. (1983). Pastoralism yesterday and today: the overgrazing problem. Pp. 643-66 in BOURLIERE (Ed.).

Lanly, J. (1982). *Tropical Forest Resources.* UN-FAO, Rome, Italy.

Lehmkuhl, J. F., Upreti, R. K. and Sharma, U. R. (1988). National parks and local development: grasses and people in Royal Chitwan National Park, Nepal. *Environmental Conservation,* 15, pp. 143-48.

Little, P. D. (1981). *A Socioecological Report on the Il Chamus of Baringo District, Kenya.* Consultant Report to Baringo Semi-Arid Area Project. Ministry of Agriculture, Nairobi.

Lusigi, W. J. (1984). Future directions for the Afro-tropical realm. Pp. 37-146 in MCNEELY and MILLER (Eds.).

Lusigi, W. J. (1981). New approaches to wildlife conservation in Kenya. *Ambio,* 10, pp. 87-92.

Machlis, G. E. and Tichnell, D. L. (1987). Economic development and threats to national parks: a preliminary analysis. *Environmental Conservation,* 14, pp. 151-6.

MacKinnon, J., MacKinnon, K., Child, G. and Thorsell, J. (1986). *Managing Protected Areas in the Tropics.* IUCN Publication, Gland, Switzerland.

Magurran, A. E. (1988). *Ecological Diversity and its Measurement*. Croom Helm, Sydney, Australia.

Mahat, T. B. S. (1987). *Forestry-Farming Linkages in the Mountains*. International Centre for Integrated Mountain Development, Kathmandu, Nepal.

Mahendra, A. K., Rai, M. P. and Rawat, J. K. (1992). Forest for energy in rural economy. *Indian Forester*, 118, pp. 256-59.

Maikhuri, R. K. (1991). Fuelwood consumption pattern of different tribal communities living in Arunachal Pradesh in North East India. *Bioresource Techno*, 35, pp. 291-6.

Maithani, G. P., Mishra, N. M. and Mahendra, A. K. (1986). Socio-economic factors associated with fuel consumption in rural areas (Village- Karaundi). *Indian Forester*, 112, pp. 753-61.

Malhotra, K. C. (1993). *Role of NTFPs in Village Economies*. ODI Network Paper.

Mayer, A. C. (1975). On becoming a participant observer. Pp. 27-41 in BÉTEILLE and MADAN (Eds.).

Mayer, A. C. (1960). *Caste and Kinship in Central India*. University of California Press. Berkley and Los Angeles, USA.

McCay, B. M. and Acheson, J. M. (Eds.)(1987). *The Question of the Commons*. University of Arizona Press, Tucson.

McNeely, J. A. (1990). How conservation strategies contribute to sustainable development. *Environmental Conservation*, 17, pp. 9-13.

McNeely, J. A. and Miller, K. R. (Eds.)(1984). *National Parks, Conservation and Development: The Role of Protected Areas in Sustaining Society.* Smithsonian Institution Press, Washington, D.C., USA.

McNeely, J. A. (1988). *Economics and Biological Diversity: Developing and Using Economic Incentives to Conserve Biological Diversity.* IUCN, Gland, Switzerland.

Miller, K. R. (1984). The Bali Action Plan: a framework for the future of protected areas. Pp. 756-64 in MCNEELY and MILLER (Eds.).

Milton, J. P. and Binney, G. A. (1980). *Ecological Planning in the Nepalese Terai: A Report on Resolving Resource Conflicts Between Wildlife Conservation and Agricultural Land-use in Padampur Panchayat.* Threshold International Centre for Environmental Renewal, Washington D.C., USA.

Mishra, H. R. (1982). Balancing human needs and conservation in Nepal's Royal Chitwan Park. *Ambio*, 11, pp. 246-51.

Mishra, H. R. (1984). A delicate balance: tigers, rhinoceros, tourists and park management vs the needs of local people in Royal Chitwan Park. Pp. 197-205 in McNEELY and MILLER (Eds.).

Mishra, S. (1999). Ritual tribal hunt has forest officials in a tizzy. *Hindustan Times*, April 4, pp. 10.

Mishra, B. K. and Ramakrishnan, P. S. (1982). Energy flow through a village ecosystem with slash and burn agriculture in north- eastern India. *Agricultural Systems*, 9, pp. 57-72.

Misra, N. M., Mahendra, A. K. and Ansari, M. Y. (1988). Pilot survey of fuel consumption in rural areas-V. *Indian Forester*, 114, pp. 57-62.

Moench, M. (1989). Forest degradation and the structure of biomass utilization   in a Himalayan foothills village. *Environmental Conservation*, 16, pp. 137-46.

Mohapatra, S. (1999). Rapid depletion of forests worries conservationists. *Hindustan Times*, March 8, pp. 24.

Morgan, R. P. C. (Ed.)(1980). *Soil Conservation: Problems and Prospects*. Wiley, Chichester, England, U.K.

Murthy, K. S. D. (1999). They prefer death to eviction. *Hindustan Times*, May 1, pp.1.

Musavi, A., Mathur, P. K., Qureishi, Q. and Sawarkar, V. B. (2006). Mapping of biotic pressure and its impact on prey densities in Melghat Tiger Reserve, Maharashtra. *International Journal of Ecology and Environmental Sciences,* 32(4): pp. 327-343.

Myres, N. (1981). A farewell to Africa. *National Wildlife*, 11, pp. 36-46.

Negi, Y. S., Sharma, L. R. and Singh, J. (1986). Factors affecting fuelwood consumption- a micro-level study. *Indian Forester*, 112, pp. 737-741.

Nelson, J. G. (1978). International experience with national parks and related reserves. Pp.1-27 in NELSON, NEEDHAM and MANN (Eds.).

Nelson, J. G., Needham, R. D. and Mann, D. L. (Eds.) (1978). *International Experience with National Parks and Related Reserves*. Department of Geography, University of Waterloo, Ontario, Canada.

Nepal, S. K. and Weber, K. E. (1993). *Struggle for Existence: Park-People Conflict in the Royal Chitwan National Park, Nepal*. HSD Monograph, 28. Division of Human Settlements Development, Asian Institute of Technology, Bangkok, Thailand.

Nepal, S. K. and Weber, K. E. (1994). A buffer zone for biodiversity conservation: viability of the concept in Nepal's Royal Chitwan National Park. *Environmental Conservation*, 21, pp. 333-41.

NES (1992). *Bhutan: Towards Sustainable Development in a Unique Environment*. Thimpu, Bhutan.

Newmark, W. D., Leonard, N. L. Sariko, H. I. and Gamassa, D. M. (1993). Conservation attitudes of local people living adjacent to five protected areas in Tanzania. *Biological Conservation*, 63, pp. 177-83.

Openshaw, K. (1980). Woodfuel- a time for reassessment. Pp. 72-86 in SMIL and KNOWLAND (Eds.).

Orsdol, K. G. V. (1987). *Buffer Zone Agroforestry in Tropical Forest Regions.* USDA Office of International Cooperation and USDA Forestry Service, Washington, D.C., USA.

Osemeobo, G. J. (1988). The human causes of forest depletion in Nigeria. *Environmental Conservation,* 15, pp. 17-28.

Pant, M. M. (1977). Forestry sector - its contribution to gross national product. *Indian Forester,* 103, pp. 739-69.

Panwar, H. S. (1990). *Status of Management of Protected Areas in India: Problems and Prospects.* Presented at the Regional Expert Consultation on Management of Protected Areas in the Asia-Pacific Region organised by FAO Regional Office for Asia and the Pacific, Bangkok, Thailand, 10-14 Dec., 1990.

Panwar, H. S. (1992). *Ecodevelopment: An Integrated Approach to Sustainable Development for People and Protected Areas in India.* Paper presented in IV World Congress on National Parks and Protected Areas, 10-12 February, 1992, Caracas, Venezuela.

Panwar, H. S. (1982). What do you do when you've succeeded: Project Tiger ten years later. *Ambio,* 11, pp. 330-37.

Park, J. E. and Park, K. (1991). *Textbook of Preventive and Social Medicine,* 13th edition. Banarsidas Bharat Publishers, Jabalpur, India.

Patel, R. I. (1982). *Forest Flora of Melghat*. Dehradun, India.

Pearce, D., Barbier, E. and Markandya, A. (1990). *Sustainable Development: Economics and Environment in the Third World*. Billing and Sons, Worcester, England, UK.

Pearce, D. W. (1975). *The Economics of Natural Resource Depletion*. Macmillan, London, England, UK.

Perrings, C. A., Maler, K. G., Folke, C., Holling, C. S. and Jansson, B. O. (Eds.)(1995). *Biodiversity Conservation: Policy, Issues and Options*. Dordrecht, the Netherlands: Kluwer Academic Press.

Perrings, C. A. (1987). *Economy and Environment: A Theoretical Essay on the Interdependence of Economic and Environmental Systems.* Cambridge University Press, New York, NY, USA: 192 pp.

Phythian-Adams, E. G. (1939). The Nilgiri Game Association 1879-1939. *Journal of Bombay Natural History Society*, 41, pp. 374-96.

Pinkerton, E. (1987). Intercepting the State: Dramatic Processes in Assertion of Local Comanagement Rights. Pp. 344-69 in McCAY and ACHESON(Eds.).

Ponting, C. (1990). Historical perspectives on sustainable development. *Environment*, 32, pp. 4-9.

Purohit, M. L. and Trivedi, H. A. S. (1991). Human factors and fuel wood consumption in Barmenr district of Western Rajasthan. *Trans Indian Soc. Desert Techno,* 16, pp. 7-14.

Radcliffe-Brown, A. R. (1979). *Structure and Function in Primitive Society.* Routlege and Kegan Paul, London and Henley, UK.

Ranjan, S. K. (1986). *Animal Nutrition and Feeding Practices.* Vikash Publishing, New Delhi, India.

Rao, K.(unpublished data). *Management problem: people in protected areas.*

Raval, S. R. (1991). The Gir National Park and the Maldharis: beyond "setting aside". Pp. 68-85 in WEST and BRECHIN (Eds.).

Repetto, R. (1992). Accounting for environmental assets. *Scientific American,* 266, pp. 94-100.

Rodgers, W. A. (unpublished data). *Wildlife conservation in India in the twenty-first century: planning a protected area network that is biologically adequate and socially acceptable.*

Rodgers, W. A. and Panwar, H. S. (1988). *Planning a Wildlife Protected Area Network in India.* Wildlife Institute of India, FAO Project. Vol. I & II, Wildlife Institute of India's Publication, Dehra Dun, India.

Rodgers, W. A. (1991). Information and professional protected area management. *Parks,* 2, pp. 4-8.

Russell, R. V. and Lal, R. B. H. (1975). The Tribes and Castes of the Central Provinces of India. Vol. I-IV. Rajdhani Book Centre, Delhi, India.

Sagar, S. R., Chandola, L. P. and Ansari, M. Y. (1981). Pilot survey of fuel consumption in rural area-II. *Indian Forester*, 107, pp. 486-91.

Saharia, V. B. (1984). Human dimensions in wildlife management: the Indian experience. Pp. 190-7 in McNEELY and MILLER (Eds.).

Sandford, S. (1983). *Management of Pastoral Development in the Third World*. Chichester, Wiley.

Sarabhai, K. V., Bhatt, S., Khacher, L., Raju, G. and Vaishnav, M. N. (1991). *People's involvement in wildlife management: an approach to joint sanctuary management of the Shoolpaneshwar Sanctuary, Gujarat*. Viksat, Ahmedabad. An approach paper prepared for the World Bank.

Sarin, S. and and Khanna, A. (1981). *Commercialisation of MFPs. Case of Sal seeds. Imperatives for future*. Xavier Labour Relations Institute, Jamshedpur, India.

Sarin, S. (1981). Management of minor forestry produce: perspective and alternative frameworks for research and analysis. *Indian Forester*, 107, pp. 397-411.

Sawarkar, V. B. and Panwar, H. S. (1987). *Integrated strategy for conservation-The Satpura case*. IV International Symposium on Tropical Ecology, Varanasi, 11-16 Dec., 1987.

Sawarkar, V.B. and V. Uniyal (unpublished data). *Landscape Diversity: Satpura Hills, India.*

Sawarkar, V. B. (1979). *Study of some aspects of predation on domestic livestock by tiger in Melghat Tiger Reserve.* Proceedings of International Symposium on Tigers, N. Delhi.

Sawarkar, V.B., Mathur, P.K. & Musavi, A. (2000). Developing area specific management guidelines for conservation of biodiversity, taking into consideration the existing forestry practices and local people's needs – A socio-economic study of triabals and non-tribals in Melgaht Tiger Reserve and Bori Wildife Sanctuary. Project Report, Wildlife Institute of India, Dehradun, India. Pp.184.

Saxena, K. P. and Singh, J. S. (1982). A phytosociological analysis of woody species in forest communities of a part of Kumaon Himalayas. *Vegetatio,* 50, pp. 3-22.

Sayer, J. (1991). Buffer zone management in rain forest protected areas. *Tiger Paper,* 18, pp. 10-17.

Schelhas, J. (1991). A methodology for assessment of external issues facing national parks with an application in Costa Rica. *Environmental Conservation,* 18, pp. 323-30.

Shah, A. M. (1964). Basic terms and concepts in the study of family in India. *Indian Economic and Social Review,* 1, pp. 1-36.

_____**(1968).** Changes in the Indian family: an examination of some assumptions. *Economic and Political Weekly*, 3, pp. 127-34.

_____**(1973).***The Household Dimension of the Family in India*. Orient Longman, Delhi, India.

_____**(1996).** Is the joint household disintegrating? *Economic and Political Weekly*, March 2, pp. 537-42.

Sharma, S. P. (1987). Energy pricing issues in Nepal. Pp. 103-36 in KUMAR (Ed.).

Sharma, U. R. and Shaw, W. W. (1993). Role of Nepal's Royal Chitwan National Park in meeting the grazing and fodder needs of local people. *Environmental Conservation*, 20, pp. 139-42.

Sheikh, M. I. (1986). Approaches to watershed management in areas affected by overgrazing and misuse of rangeland resources. Pp. 85-100 in Integrated Watershed Management. UN FAO, Rome, Italy.

Shelton, N. (1983). Parks and sustainable development. 1982 World National Parks Congress, pp. 16-21. *National Parks.*

Simon, D. (1989). Sustainable development: theoretical construct or attainable goal? *Environmental Conservation*, 16, pp.41-48.

Singer, M. and Cohn, B. S. (Eds.)(1968). *Structure and Change in Indian Society.* Aldine Publishing Company, Chicago, USA.

Singh, A. (1981). Wood as source of energy for rural communities. *Indian Forester*, 107, pp. 115-23.

Singh, K. P. and Singh, J. S. (1988). Certain structural and functional aspects of dry tropical forest and savanna. *International Journal of Ecology and Environmental Sciences*, 14, pp. 31-45.

Singh, V. P. and Singh, J. S. (1989). Man and forests: a case study of the dry tropics of India. *Environmental Conservation*, 16, pp. 129-36.

Smiet, A. C. (1990). Agroforestry and fuelwood in Jawa. *Environmental Conservation*, 17, pp. 235-8.

Smil, V. and Knowland, W. (Eds.)(1980). *Energy in a Developing World*. Oxford University Press, New York, NY, USA.

Stracey, P. D. (1963). *Wildlife in India. Its Conservation and Control*. Department of Agriculture, New Delhi, India.

Sunderlin, W. D., Angelsen, A., Belcher, B. Burgers, P., Nasi, R., Santoso, L. & Wunder, S. (2005) Livelihoods, Forests, and Conservation in Developing Countries: An Overview. *World Development* **33(9):** 1383-1402.

Talbot, L. M. and Olindo, P. (1990). The Maasai Mara and Amboseli Reserves, Kenya. Pp. 67-84 in KISS (Ed.).

Tewari, D. N. (1991). Forest and tribal. *Indian Forester*, 117, pp. 984-89.

Thapa, G. B. and Weber, K. E. (1988). *Land Settlement in Tropical Asia: Prospects for an Alternative Planning strategy.* Asian Institute of Technology, Bangkok, Thailand.

Thapa, G. B. and Weber, K. E. (1990). Actors and factors of deforestation in Tropical Asia, *Environmental Conservation*, 17, pp. 19-27.

Thapa, G. B. and Weber, K. E. (1991). Deforestation in the Upper Pokhara Valley, Nepal. *Singapore Journal of Tropical Geography*, 12, pp. 52-67.

Thapa, G. B. and Weber, K. E. (1994). Prospects of private forestry around urban centres: a study of Upland Nepal. *Environmental Conservation*, 21, pp. 297-307.

Tucker, R. P. (1991). Resident peoples and wildlife reserves in India: the prehistory of a strategy. Pp. 40-50 in WEST, and BRECHIN (Eds.).

Uhlig, H. (Ed.)(1984). *Spontaneous and Planned Settlement in Southeast Asia.* Institute of Asian Affairs, Hamburg, W. Germany.

Upreti, G. (1987). Ecological problems and conservation needs. *The Rising Nepal*, Feb.,18, pp. 2-3.

Upreti, G. (1994). Environmental conservation and sustainable development require a new development approach. *Environmental Conservation*, 21, pp. 18-29.

Wallace, M. (1981). *Solving Common Property Resources Problems: Deforestation in Nepal.* PhD. thesis, Harvard University, Cambridge, Massachusetts, USA.

Wankhade, R. K. and Mahajan, A. G. (1992). Dimensions of domestic livestock predation by tigers and leopards in Melghat Tiger Reserve. Pp. 81-9 in GOGATE, THOSARE, and BANUBAKODE (Eds.).

Wells, M. P. (1995). Biodiversity conservation and local development aspirations: new priorities for the 1990s. In PERRINGS, MALER, FOLKE, HOLLING and JANSSON (Eds.).

Wells, M. P. and Brandon, K. E. (1993). The principles and practice of buffer zones and local participation in biodiversity conservation. *Ambio*, 22, pp. 157-62.

Wells, M. P., Brandon, K. E. and Hannah, L. J. (1992). *People and Parks, Linking Protected Area Management with Local Communities.* World Bank, Washington D.C., USA.

Weninger, M. (1952). Anthropologische Untersuchungen and einigen Staemmen Zentralindiens. *Acta Ethnologica et Linguistica*, Band 3, Vienna.

West, P. C. and Brechin S. R. (Eds.)(1991). *Resident Peoples and National Parks: Social Dilemmas and Strategies in International Conservation.* Tucson: The University of Arizona Press.

Western, D. (1982). Amboseli National Park: enlisting landowners to conserve migratory wildlife. *Ambio*, 11, pp. 302-8.

World Resources (1992). *1992-93 - A Report by the World Resources Institute*. UNEP and UNDP, Oxford University Press, NY, USA.

WRI & IIED (1987). *World Resources*. New York, NY, USA.

Index

G

Game associations 3; reserve 10; regulating hunting 3.

Grazing 13, 33, 63,73, 84, 116, 134, 144

    impact 26, 27, 127 156; indiscriminate 19; intensity 107; over 26; regulate 33; signs 104; uncontrolled 26; weed 114

Gugamal National Park 36, 65, 103, 108, 115, 116, 156.

I

Indian National Parks Act 4

Indigenous communities 15, 46, 100

IUCN 7, 18, 154

L

Landlessness 12, 93

farmers 12; local communities 45.

Land-use forms of 26; policies 13; practice 10; strategy of 33; sustainable 20.

Livestock agro-pastoral 85, 96; degradation 2; free ranging 103; grazing 19, 25, 95, 99, 102, 114, 117, 123, 127, 132,150; holding 24, 26, 50 94; ownership 74; predation 33; stored wealth 99; waterhole use 123.

Local people 2, 11, 13-20, 24, 30, 32, 52, 68, 90, 91, 93, 102, 108, 111, 112, 114, 116, 117, 119, 122, 146-149, 152, 154, 156-159, 161-164

M

Maharaja of Kashmir 4

Marginalisation 12, 45, 46

Melghat Tiger Reserve 32, 37, 39

fauna 43; forests 36, 38, 42, 108; Korkus 33; predation 33; villages 65

N

National Park 4, 7, 8, 9

administrative zones 122; boundary 137, 138; data for 105.

National Wildlife Board 5

Natural resources 6

degradation 6; rural society 6; water regime 6; over-exploitation 6.

Non-timber forest product (NTFP)

collection 28, 51, 54, 57, 63, 73, 80, 82, 95, 96, 99, 111, 116; contribution to household income 24, 98; dependence on 24, 96, 99, 163; employment generation 24, 25;

forest exploitation 13; major resource 24; management of 24; marketing of 25; role of women 28; sale of 24, 56, 57, 73, 79, 98, 99; species 118, 119.

P

Panchmarhi Wildife Sanctuary 38

Preservation of natural ecological processes 7; biologically important areas 36.

Project Tiger 5

Protected Area 2, 7, 13, 37, 51, 82, 100, 102, 121, 146, 149, 154

benefits 7, 20; categories 7; definition 5; dependence 46; eco-development 20; ecological studies 31; human presence 4; local communities 30;

countries 11, 25, 26; India
101; Moist 12.

Printed in the United States
By Bookmasters